Cecil Frances Alexander

The Sunday book of poetry

Cecil Frances Alexander

The Sunday book of poetry

ISBN/EAN: 9783744744775

Printed in Europe, USA, Canada, Australia, Japan

Cover: Foto ©Thomas Meinert / pixelio.de

More available books at **www.hansebooks.com**

The Sunday Book of Poetry

THE SUNDAY BOOK OF POETRY

SELECTED AND ARRANGED BY

C. F. ALEXANDER

AUTHOR OF "HYMNS FOR LITTLE CHILDREN," ETC.

London
MACMILLAN AND CO.
AND NEW YORK
1887

LONDON:
Printed by RICHARD CLAY AND SONS, 1864.
Reprinted 1865, 1872, 1876, 1878, 1882, 1887.

PREFACE

THE present volume will, it is hoped, be found to contain a selection of Sacred Poetry, of such a character as can be placed with profit and pleasure in the hands of intelligent children from eight to fourteen years of age, both on Sundays and at other times.

It may be well for the Compiler to make some remarks upon the principles which have been adopted in the present selection.

Dr. Johnson has said that "the word Sacred should never be applied but where some reference may be made to a higher Being, or where some duty is exacted, or implied." The Compiler believes she has selected few poems whose insertion may not be justified by this definition, though several perhaps may not be of such a nature as are popularly termed *sacred*. Those which appear under the division of the Incarnate Word, and of Praise, and Prayer, are of course in some cases directly hymns, and in all cases founded upon the great doctrines of the Christian faith, or upon the events of the Redeemer's life. Many of the poems under the head of the Written Word, and indeed in all the divisions, are of an equally decided religious character. But in illustrating some passages of Holy Scripture, in delineating the various phases and duties of life, in tracing out the hopes and fears which encompass death, in picturing the feelings and passions of the human heart, she has freely availed herself of pieces whose tendency is moral and elevating, though the language may not be directly religious.

The Compiler has selected freely from our English Poets, ancient and modern, and she believes that there is scarcely one of high note who is not represented in the present collection. She hopes that it may be thus, in some sort, a kind of informal introduction to the highest works of English literature. It might be thought that pieces from writers so diverse as Milton and Keble, Toplady and Crashaw, Heber and Bonar, must necessarily contain heterogeneous doctrine; but it will be found that these poems, from so many writers of different schools, contain nothing which is not in accordance with those great truths of the Gospel of Christ, "which are most surely believed among us." It was remarked at the Great Exhibition, that the works of all Christian lands bore a family likeness. Is it strange that a finer and closer family likeness should be found in the works of Christian men and women, hymning the same Incarnate Lord, and contemplating life, death, and nature, from so many common points of view?

It is possible that some persons may consider many of the poems in the present volume too difficult for children of the ages indicated. The Compiler is assured, however, by actual experiment, that there is little, if anything, in the entire collection, which is not capable of giving pleasure to such children, if they are of ordinary intelligence. A namby-pamby, childish style is most unpleasing to children, especially to boys; it is surprising how soon they can understand and follow a high order of poetry (always supposing it is not subtle or metaphysical), especially when it assumes a narrative form, and has the aid of rhyme.

The Compiler is, as a general rule, most averse to the practice of garbling or altering poems. A rash collector may work as blindly with a fine poem as a rash restorer with a fine picture ; but the exigencies of children's tastes and capacities, and the necessary limits of the work, have required frequent abbreviation. Thus, in selecting from the works of Wordsworth, and the great author of " The Christian Year," she has sometimes taken a single thought or picture detached from the context, having to make her choice between this course or the omission of some of the holiest and loveliest lines in English sacred song. Once or twice only she has altered a word, or transposed a line for the sake of connexion, or changed into modern language the obsolete expressions of some very old writer.

The Compiler cannot close her task without the prayer that this volume may in some measure tend to make Sunday a pleasant day to children. May it help to teach them to praise God the Father, Son, and Spirit; to contemplate life and death and their own hearts as Christians should: to understand the spirit of the Bible; and through this fair creation to look up to Him who is its Creator.

C. F. ALEXANDER.

The Sunday Book of Poetry for the Young

I

PRAYER

Prayer is the soul's sincere desire,
   Utter'd, or unexpress'd ;
The motion of a hidden fire
   That trembles in the breast.

Prayer is the burthen of a sigh,
   The falling of a tear,
The upward glancing of the eye,
   When none but God is near.

Prayer is the simplest form of speech
   That infant lips can try ;
Prayer the sublimest strains that reach
   The Majesty on high.

Prayer is the contrite sinner's voice
   Returning from his ways,
While angels in their songs rejoice,
   And cry, Behold he prays !

Prayer is the Christian's vital breath,
  The Christian's native air;
His watchword at the gates of death;
  He enters Heaven with prayer.

The saints, in prayer, appear as one
  In word, and deed, and mind,
While with the Father and the Son
  Sweet fellowship they find.

Nor prayer is made by man alone,
  The Holy Spirit pleads;
And Jesus, on th' eternal throne,
  For sinners intercedes.

O Thou, by whom we come to God!
  The Life, the Truth, the Way!
The path of prayer Thyself hast trod:
  Lord! teach us how to pray.
                    J. Montgomery

II

PSALM CXLVIII

Come, O! come, with sacred lays,
Let us sound th' Almighty's praise;
Hither, bring in true consent,
Heart, and voice, and instrument.
Let the orpharion sweet
With the harp and viol meet:

Book of Poetry

To your voices tune the lute:
Let not tongue nor string be mute:
Nor a creature dumb be found,
That hath either voice or sound.

Let such things as do not live,
In still music praises give ;
Lowly pipe, ye worms that creep
On the earth, or in the deep ;
Loud aloft your voices strain,
Beasts and monsters of the main ;
Birds, your warbling treble sing ;
Clouds, your peals of thunder ring ;
Sun and Moon exalted higher,
And you Stars, augment the quire.

Come, ye sons of human race,
In this chorus take your place,
And amid this mortal throng,
Be ye masters of the song.
Angels and celestial powers,
Be the noblest tenor yours.
Let, in praise of God, the sound
Run a never-ending round,
That our holy hymn may be
Everlasting, as is He.

From the earth's vast hollow womb
Music's deepest bass shall come,
Sea and floods from shore to shore
Shall the counter-tenor roar.
To this concert, when we sing,
Whistling winds, your descant bring :

Which may bear the sound above
Where the orb of fire doth move;
And so climb from sphere to sphere,
Till our song th' Almighty hear.

So shall He from Heaven's high tower
On the earth His blessing shower;
All this huge wide orb we see
Shall one choir, one temple be;
There our voices we will rear
Till we fill it everywhere:
And enforce the fiends that dwell
In the air, to sink to hell.
Then, O! come, with sacred lays,
Let us sound th' Almighty's praise.
G. Wither

III

HYMN OF PRAISE

Holy, holy, holy, Lord,
  God of Hosts! When heaven and earth
Out of darkness, at Thy Word,
  Issued into glorious birth,
All Thy works before Thee stood,
And Thine eye beheld them good,
While they sang with one accord,
  Holy, holy, holy, Lord!

Holy, holy, holy! Thee
  One Jehovah evermore
Father, Son, and Spirit, we,
  Dust and ashes, would adore:

Lightly by the world esteem'd,
From that world by Thee redeem'd,
Sing we here, with glad accord,
   Holy, holy, holy, Lord!

Holy, holy, holy! all
   Heaven's triumphant choir shall sing,
When the ransom'd nations fall
   At the footstool of their King:
Then shall saints and seraphim,
Hearts and voices, swell one hymn,
Round the throne with full accord,
   Holy, holy, holy, Lord!

J. Montgomery

IV

THE GOODNESS OF GOD

Yes, God is good: in earth and sky,
   From ocean-depths and spreading wood,
Ten thousand voices seem to cry,
   "God made us all, and God is good."

The sun that keeps his trackless way,
   And downward pours his golden flood,
Night's sparkling hosts, all seem to say,
   In accents clear, that God is good.

The merry birds prolong the strain,
   Their song with every spring renew'd;
And balmy air, and falling rain,
   Each softly whisper, "God is good."

I hear it in the rushing breeze;
  The hills that have for ages stood,
The echoing sky, and roaring seas,
  All swell the chorus, "God is good."

Yes, God is good, all Nature says,
  By God's own hand with speech endued;
And man, in louder notes of praise,
  Should sing for joy that "God is good."

For all Thy gifts we bless Thee, Lord,
  But chiefly for our heavenly food,
Thy pardoning grace, Thy quick'ning word;
  These prompt our song that "God is good."

J. H. Gurney

V

THE GOODNESS OF PROVIDENCE

The Lord my pasture shall prepare,
And feed me with a shepherd's care;
His presence shall my wants supply,
And guard me with a watchful eye;
My noon-day walks He shall attend,
And all my midnight hours defend.

When in the sultry glebe I faint,
Or on the thirsty mountains pant,
To fertile vales, and dewy meads,
My weary wandering steps He leads,

Where peaceful rivers, soft and slow,
Amid the verdant landscape flow.

Though in the paths of death I tread,
With gloomy horror overspread,
My stedfast heart shall fear no ill :
For Thou, O Lord, art with me still :
Thy friendly crook shall give me aid,
And guide me through the dreadful shade.

Though in a bare and rugged way,
Through devious lonely wilds I stray,
Thy bounty shall my pains beguile ;
The barren wilderness shall smile,
With sudden greens, and herbage crown'd,
And streams shall murmur all around.

J. Addison

VI

HYMN TO GOD THE FATHER

Hear me, O God !
A broken heart
Is my best part :
Use still Thy rod,
  That I may prove
  Therein Thy love.

If Thou hadst not
  Been stern to me,
  But left me free,
I had forgot
  Myself and Thee.

For sin's so sweet,
  As minds ill-bent
  Rarely repent,
Until they meet
  Their punishment.

Ben Jonson

VII

PROVIDENCE

God moves in a mysterious way
  His wonders to perform;
He plants his footsteps in the sea,
  And rides upon the storm.

Deep in unfathomable mines
  Of never-failing skill,
He treasures up His bright designs,
  And works his sovereign will.

Ye fearful saints, fresh courage take,
  The clouds ye so much dread
Are big with mercy, and shall break
  In blessings on your head.

Judge not the Lord by feeble sense,
  But trust Him for His grace;
Behind a frowning Providence
  He hides a smiling face.

His purposes will ripen fast,
   Unfolding every hour;
The bud may have a bitter taste,
   But sweet will be the flower.

Blind unbelief is sure to err,
   And scan His work in vain;
God is His own interpreter,
   And He will make it plain.
                              W. Cowper

VIII

THE EMIGRANTS SACRED SONG

Where the remote Bermudas ride
In ocean's bosom unespied,
From a small boat that row'd along,
The listening winds received their song.

" What should we do but sing His praise
That led us through the watery maze,
Unto an isle so long unknown,
And yet far kinder than our own.

" Where He the huge sea-monsters racks,
That lift the deep upon their backs ;
He lands us on a grassy stage,
Safe from the storm's and tyrant's rage.

" He gave us this eternal spring
Which here enamels every thing,
And sends the fowls to us in care,
On daily visits through the air.

" He hangs in shades the orange bright,
Like golden lamps in a green night,
And in these rocks for us did frame
A temple where to sound His name.

"Oh ! let our voice His praise exalt
Till it arrive at Heaven's vault,
Which then perhaps rebounding may
Echo beyond the Mexique bay."

Thus sang they in the English boat,
A holy and a cheerful note,
And all the way, to guide their chime,
With falling oars they kept the time.
A. Marvel

IX

THE LOVE OF GOD

Blest be Thy love, dear Lord,
  That taught us this sweet way
Only to love Thee for Thyself,
  And for that love obey.

O Thou, our soul's chief hope !
  We to thy mercy fly;
Where'er we are, Thou canst protect,
  Whate'er we need, supply.

Whether we sleep or wake,
  To Thee we both resign;
By night we see, as well as day,
  If Thy light on us shine.

Whether we live, or die,
Both we submit to Thee;
In death we live, as well as life,
If Thine in death we be.
J. Austin

X

GOD THE ONLY COMFORTER

O Thou that driest the mourner's tear,
   How dark this world would be,
If, when deceived and wounded here,
   We could not fly to Thee!

The friends who in our sunshine live,
   When winter comes are flown;
And he who has but tears to give,
   Must weep those tears alone.

But Thou wilt heal the broken heart,
   Which, like the plants that throw
Their fragrance from the wounded part,
   Breathes sweetness out of woe.

When joy no longer soothes, or cheers,
   And even the hope that threw
A moment's sparkle o'er our tears,
   Is dimmed and vanish'd too!

Oh! who could bear life's stormy doom,
   Did not Thy wing of love
Come brightly wafting through the gloom,
   One peace-branch from above?

Then sorrow touch'd by Thee grows bright
   With more than rapture's ray;
As darkness shows us worlds of light
   We could not see by day.
T. Moore

XI

A PRAYER

Imitated from the Persian

Lord! who art merciful as well as just,
Incline Thine ear to me, a child of dust!
Not what I would, O Lord! I offer Thee,
   Alas! but what I can.
Father Almighty, who hast made me man,
And bade me look to heaven, for Thou art there,
Accept my sacrifice and humble prayer.
Four things which are not in Thy treasury,
I lay before Thee, Lord, with this petition:
   My nothingness, my wants,
   My sins, and my contrition.
R. Southey

XII

THY WILL BE DONE

Father, I know that all my life
   Is portion'd out for me,
And the changes that are sure to come
   I do not fear to see;
But I ask Thee for a present mind,
   Intent on pleasing Thee.

I ask Thee for a thoughtful love,
   Thro' constant watching wise,
To meet the glad with joyful smiles
   And wipe the weeping eyes:
And a heart at leisure from itself,
   To soothe and sympathise.

I would not have the restless will
   That hurries to and fro ;
Seeking for some great thing to do,
   A secret thing to know :
I would be treated as a child,
   And guided where I go.

Wherever in the world I am,
   In whatsoe'er estate,
I have a fellowship with hearts
   To keep and cultivate,
And a work of lowly love to do,
   From the Lord on whom I wait.

And if some things I do not ask
   In my cup of blessing be,
I would have my spirit fill'd the more
   With grateful love to Thee ;
More careful, not to serve Thee much,
   But to please Thee perfectly.

There are briars besetting every path
   That call for patient care ;
There is a cross in every lot,
   And an earnest need for prayer;
But a lowly heart, that leans on Thee,
   Is happy anywhere.

In a service which Thy will appoints,
    There are no bonds for me ;
For my inmost heart is taught the truth
    That makes Thy children free :
And a life of self-renouncing love
    Is a life of liberty.

A. L. Waring

XIII

THE FORCE OF PRAYER

"What is good for a bootless bene ?"
    With these dark words begins my tale ;
And their meaning is, whence can comfort spring
    When prayer is of no avail ?

"What is good for a bootless bene ?"
    The falconer to the lady said ;
And she made answer, " Endless sorrow ! "
    For she knew that her son was dead.

She knew it by the falconer's words,
    And from the look of the falconer's eye ;
And from the love that was in her soul
    For her youthful Romilly.

Young Romilly through Barden woods
    Is ranging high and low ;
And holds a greyhound in a leash
    To let slip upon buck or doe.

The pair have reach'd that fearful chasm,
   How tempting to bestride !
For lordly Wharf is there pent in
   With rocks on either side.

This striding place is called the Strid,
   A name which it took of yore :
A thousand years hath it borne that name,
   And shall a thousand more.

And hither is young Romilly come,
   And what may now forbid,
That he, perhaps for the hundredth time,
   Shall bound across the Strid ?

He sprang in glee—for what cared he
   That the river was strong and the rocks were steep?
But the greyhound in the leash hung back,
   And check'd him in his leap.

The boy is in the arms of Wharf,
   And strangled by a merciless force ;
For never more was young Romilly seen
   Till he rose a lifeless corse.

Now there is stillness in the vale,
   And long unspeaking sorrow :
Wharf shall be to pitying hearts
   A name more sad than Yarrow.

Long, long in darkness did she sit,
   And her first words were, " Let there be,
In Bolton, on the field of Wharf,
   A stately Priory."

The stately Priory was rear'd,
  And Wharf as he roll'd along
To matins join'd a mournful voice,
  Nor fail'd at even-song.

And the Lady pray'd in heaviness
  That look'd not for relief!
But slowly did her succour come,
  And a patience to her grief.

Oh there is never sorrow of heart,
  That shall lack a timely end,
If but to God we turn, and ask
  Of Him to be our friend.
                    W. Wordsworth

XIV

THE CHRISTIAN'S PRAYER

  Jesus, my strength, my hope,
    On Thee I cast my care,
With humble confidence look up,
    And know thou hear'st my prayer.
    Give me on Thee to wait
    Till I can all things do,
  On Thee Almighty to create,
    Almighty to renew!

    I want a sober mind,
    A self-renouncing will,
That tramples down and casts behind
    The baits of pleasing ill:

A soul inured to pain,
  To hardships, grief, and loss;
Bold to take up, firm to sustain,
  The consecrated cross.

I want a godly fear,
  A quick discerning eye,
That looks to Thee when sin is near,
  That sees the tempter fly;
  A spirit still prepared,
  And arm'd with jealous care,
For ever standing on its guard,
  And watching unto prayer.

I want a heart to pray,
  To pray and never cease,
Never to murmur at Thy stay,
  Or wish my sufferings less;
  This blessing, above all,
  Always to pray, I want,
Out of the deep on Thee to call
  And never, never faint.

I want a true regard,
  A single, steady aim,
Unmoved by theat'ning, or reward,
  To Thee and Thy great name;
  A jealous, just concern
  For Thine immortal praise;
A pure desire that all may learn
  And glorify Thy grace.

I rest upon Thy word;
  Thy promise is for me;

My succour and salvation, Lord,
   Shall surely come from Thee.
   But let me still abide,
   Nor from Thy hope remove,
Till Thou my patient spirit guide
   Into Thy perfect love!
Charles Wesley

XV
THOUGHTS OF CHRIST

Jesu, the very thought of Thee
   With sweetness fills the breast;
But sweeter far Thy face to see,
   And in Thy presence rest.

No voice can sing, no heart can frame,
   Nor can the memory find,
A sweeter sound than Jesu's name,
   The Saviour of mankind.

O hope of every contrite heart,
   O joy of all the meek,
To those who fall how kind Thou art,
   How good to those who seek!

But what to those who find? Ah! this
   Nor tongue nor pen can show;
The love of Jesus, what it is,
   None but His loved ones know.

Jesu, our only joy be Thou,
   As Thou our prize wilt be;
In Thee be all our glory now,
   And through eternity.
Bernard of Fontaine
Translated by E. Caswall

XVI

HYMN

For the boatmen as they approach the rapids by Heidelberg

Jesu! bless our slender boat,
    By the current swept along;
Loud its threatenings—let them not
    Drown the music of a song
Breath'd Thy mercy to implore,
Where these troubled waters roar.

Saviour, for our warning, seen
    Bleeding on that precious rood;
If, while thro' the meadows green
    Gently wound the peaceful flood,
We forgot Thee, do not Thou
Disregard Thy suppliants now!

Hither, like yon ancient tower
    Watching o'er the river's bed,
Fling the shadow of Thy power,
    Else we sleep among the dead;
Thou who trod'st the billowy sea,
Shield us in our jeopardy!

Guide our bark among the waves;
    Through the rocks our passage smooth;
Where the whirlpool frets and raves,
    Let Thy love its anger soothe:
All our hope is placed in Thee;
Miserere Domine!

W. Wordsworth

XVII

EVENING HYMN

Sun of my soul, Thou Saviour dear,
It is not night if Thou be near;
O! may no earth-born cloud arise
To hide Thee from Thy servant's eyes.

When the soft dews of kindly sleep
My wearied eyelids gently steep,
Be my last thought how sweet to rest
For ever on my Saviour's breast.

Abide with me from morn till eve,
For without Thee I cannot live;
Abide with me when night is nigh,
For without Thee I dare not die.

If some poor wandering child of Thine
Have spurn'd to-day the voice divine,
Now, Lord, the gracious work begin;
Let him no more lie down in sin.

Watch by the sick, enrich the poor
With blessings from Thy boundless store;
Be every mourner's sleep to-night,
Like infant's slumbers, pure and light.

Come near and bless us when we wake,
Ere through the world our way we take:
Till, in the ocean of Thy love,
We lose ourselves in Heaven above.

John Keble

XVIII
THE SOUL'S LITANY

In the hour of trial,
   Jesus, pray for me;
Lest, by base denial,
   I depart from Thee:
When Thou see'st me waver,
   With a look recall,
Nor, for fear or favour,
   Suffer me to fall.

With its witching pleasures,
   Would this vain world charm;
Or its sordid treasures
   Spread, to work me harm;
Bring to my remembrance
   Sad Gethsemane,
Or, in darker semblance,
   Cross-crown'd Calvary.

If with sore affliction
   Thou in love chastise,
Pour Thy benediction
   On the sacrifice;
Then upon Thine altar,
   Freely offer'd up,
Though the flesh may falter,
   Faith shall drink the cup.

When in dust and ashes
   To the grave I sink,
While heaven's glory flashes
   O'er the shelving brink,

On Thy truth relying
  Through the mortal strife,
Lord, receive me dying
  To eternal life.

Anon.

XIX

CLINGING TO GOD

Nearer, my God, to Thee,
  Nearer to Thee!
E'en though it be a cross
  That raiseth me;
Still all my song shall be,
Nearer, my God, to Thee,
  Nearer to Thee.

Though like a wanderer,
  The sun gone down,
Darkness comes over me,
  My rest a stone;
Yet in my dreams I'd be
Nearer, my God, to Thee,
  Nearer to Thee.

There let my way appear
  Steps unto heaven;
All that Thou sendest me
  In mercy given;
Angels to beckon me
Nearer, my God, to Thee,
  Nearer to Thee.

Then with my waking thoughts
  Bright with Thy praise,

Out of my stony griefs
   Bethels I'll raise ;
So by my woes to be
   Nearer, my God, to Thee,
   Nearer to Thee !

And when on joyful wing
   Cleaving the sky,
Sun, moon, and stars forgot,
   Upward I fly,
Still all my song shall be,
Nearer, my God, to Thee,
   Nearer to Thee !
                              S. F. Adams

XX

A CRY

The way is long and dreary,
   The path is bleak and bare :
Our feet are worn and weary,
   But we will not despair.
More heavy was Thy burthen,
   More desolate Thy way ;
O Lamb of God, who takest
   The sin of the world away,
      Have mercy on us !

The snows lie thick around us,
   In the dark and gloomy night ;
And the tempest wails above us,
   And the stars have hid their light.

But blacker was the darkness
   Round Calvary's Cross that day ;
O Lamb of God, that takest
   The sin of the world away,
     Have mercy on us !

Our hearts are faint with sorrow,
   Heavy and sad to bear ;
For we dread the bitter morrow,
   But we will not despair :
Thou knowest all our anguish,
   And Thou wilt bid it cease ;
O Lamb of God, who takest
   The sin of the world away,
     Give us Thy peace !
A. A. Procter

XXI
GRATITUDE TO GOD

How blest Thy creature is, O God,
   When with a single eye
He views the lustre of Thy word,
   The day-spring from on high.

Through all the storms that veil the skies,
   And frown on earthly things,
The Sun of Righteousness he eyes
   With healing on His wings.

Struck by that light, the human heart,
   A barren soil no more,
Sends the sweet smell of grace abroad,
   Where serpents lurk'd before.

The glorious orb, whose golden beams
  The fruitful year control,
Since first, obedient to Thy word,
  He started from the goal,

Has cheer'd the nations with the joys
  His orient rays impart;
But, Jesus, 'tis Thy light alone
  Can shine upon the heart.
                    W. Cowper

XXII

HYMN TO THE HOLY SPIRIT

Praise be Thine, most Holy Spirit,
  Honour to Thy Holy Name!
May we love it, may we fear it!
  Set in everlasting fame.
Honour to Thee, praise, and glory,
  Comforter, inspirer, friend;
Till these troubles transitory
  End in glory without end.

By Thy hand, in secret working,
  Like a midnight of soft rain,
Seeds that lay in silence lurking,
  Spring up green, and grow amain.
Roots, which in their dusty bosoms
  Hid an age of golden days
Stirring with a cloud of blossoms,
  Clothe their barrenness for Thy praise.

As an island in a river
  Vex'd with endless rave and roar,
Keeps an inner silence ever
  On its consecrated shore,
Flower'd with flowers, and green with grasses:
  So the poor through Thee abide;
Every outer care that passes
  Deepening more the peace inside.

When our heart is faint Thou warmest,
  Justifiest our delight;
Thou our ignorance informest,
  And our wisdom shapest right;
In the hour of doubt and strife,
  Thou beginnest, and Thou endest,
All that Christians count of life.
Thos. Burridge

XXIII

LITANY TO THE HOLY SPIRIT

In the hour of my distress,
When temptations me oppress,
And when I my sins confess,
    Sweet Spirit, comfort me.

When I lie within my bed,
Sick in heart, and sick in head,
And with doubts disquieted,
    Sweet Spirit, comfort me.

When the house doth sigh, and weep,
And the world is drown'd in sleep,
Yet mine eyes the watch do keep,
    Sweet Spirit, comfort me.

When God knows I'm toss'd about
Either with despair or doubt,
Yet before the glass be out,
    Sweet Spirit, comfort me.

When the tempter me pursueth
With the sins of all my youth,
And reproves me for untruth,
    Sweet Spirit, comfort me.

When the judgment is reveal'd,
And that open'd which was seal'd,
When to Thee I have appeal'd,
    Sweet Spirit, comfort me.
                R. Herrick

XXIV

VENI CREATOR SPIRITUS

Come, Holy Ghost, our souls inspire,
And lighten with celestial fire;
Thou the Anointing Spirit art,
Who dost Thy sevenfold gifts impart.
Thy blessed unction from above
Is comfort, life, and fire of love.
Enable with perpetual light
The dulness of our blinded sight;
Anoint and cheer our soilèd face
With the abundance of Thy grace;
Keep far our foes; give peace at home;
Where Thou art guide, no ill can come.
Teach us to know the Father, Son,
And Thee of both, to be but One:

That, through the ages all along,
This may be our endless song:
" Praise to Thy eternal merit,
" Father, Son, and Holy Spirit!"
Ordination Service

XXV

THE HOLY TRINITY

Holy! Holy! Holy! Lord God Almighty!
Early in the morning our song shall rise to Thee,
Holy, Holy, Holy! Merciful and Mighty!
God in Three Persons, Blessed Trinity!

Holy! Holy! Holy! all the saints adore Thee,
Casting down their golden crowns around the glassy sea;
Cherubim and Seraphim falling down before Thee,
Which wert, and art, and evermore shall be.

Holy! Holy! Holy! though the darkness hide Thee,
Though the eye of sinful man Thy glory may not see,
Only Thou art Holy, there is none beside Thee
Perfect in Power, in Love, and Purity!

Holy! Holy! Holy! Lord God Almighty!
All Thy works shall praise Thy Name, in earth, and sky, and sea;
Holy! Holy! Holy! Merciful and Mighty,
God in Three Persons, Blessed Trinity!
Bishop Reginald Heber

XXVI

SACRED MUSIC

—To our high-raised phantasy present
That undisturbèd song of pure consent,
Aye sung before the sapphire-colour'd throne
To Him that sits thereon,
With saintly shout and solemn jubilee;
Where the bright seraphim in burning row,
Their loud uplifted angel trumpets blow;
And the cherubic host, in thousand choirs,
Touch their immortal harps of golden wires,
With those just spirits that wear victorious palms,
Hymns devout, and holy psalms,
Singing everlastingly:
That we on earth with undiscording voice,
May rightly answer that melodious noise;
As once we did, till disproportion'd sin
Jarr'd against Nature's chime, and with harsh din
Broke the fair music that all creatures made
To their great Lord, whose love their motion sway'd
In perfect diapason whilst they stood,
In first obedience and their state of good.
O, may we soon again renew that song
And keep in tune with heaven, till God ere long
To His celestial concert us unite
To live with Him, and sing in endless morn of light!
John Milton

XXVII
CHURCH MUSIC

But let my due feet never fail
To walk the studious cloisters pale,
And love the high embowèd roof
With antique pillars massy proof,
And storied windows richly dight
Casting a dim religious light;
There let the pealing organ blow
To the full-voiced choir below
In service high, and anthem clear,
As may with sweetness, thro' mine ear,
Dissolve mè into ecstasies
And bring all Heaven before mine eyes.
John Milton

XXVIII
EARTH AND HÈAVEN

The roseate hues of early dawn,
    The brightness of the day,
The crimson of the sunset sky,
    How fast they fade away!
O for the pearly gates of heaven!
    O for the golden floor!
O for the Sun of Righteousness
    That setteth nevermore!

The highest hopes we cherish here,
    How fast they tire and faint!
How many a spot defiles the robe
    That wraps an earthly saint!

O for a heart that never sins!
  O for a soul wash'd white!
O for a voice to praise our King,
  Nor weary day or night!

Here faith is ours, and heavenly hope,
  And grace to lead us higher:
But there are perfectness and peace
  Beyond our best desire.
O, by Thy love and anguish, Lord!
  O, by Thy life laid down!
O, that we fall not from Thy grace,
  Nor cast away our crown!
C. F. Alexander

XXIX

EVENING HYMN

Glory to Thee, my God, this night,
For all the blessings of the light;
Keep me, O keep me, King of kings,
Beneath Thine own Almighty wings.

Forgive me, Lord, for Thy dear Son,
The ill that I this day have done;
That with the world, myself, and Thee,
I, ere I sleep, at peace may be.

Teach me to live, that I may dread
The grave as little as my bed;
Teach me to die, that so I may
Rise glorious at the awful day.

O let my soul on Thee repose;
And may sweet sleep mine eyelids close:
Sleep, that shall me more vig'rous make
To serve my God when I awake.

If in the night I sleepless lie,
My soul with heavenly thoughts supply;
May no ill dreams disturb my rest,
No powers of darkness me molest.

Praise God, from whom all blessings flow,
Praise Him, all creatures here below;
Praise Him above, angelic host,
Praise Father, Son, and Holy Ghost!
Bishop Thomas Ken

II

THE INCARNATE WORD

XXX

THE INCARNATION OF CHRIST

For Thou wert born of woman ! Thou didst come,
O Holiest, to this world of sin and gloom,
Not in Thy dread omnipotent array ;
    And not by thunders strew'd
    Was Thy tempestuous road ;
Nor indignation burn'd before Thee on Thy way.
    But Thee, a soft and naked child,
    Thy mother undefiled
    In the rude manger laid to rest
    From off her virgin breast.

The Heavens were not commanded to prepare
A gorgeous canopy of golden air ;
Nor stoop'd their lamps th' enthronèd fires on high:
    A single silent star
    Came wand'ring from afar,
Gliding uncheck'd and calm along the liquid sky,
    The Eastern sages leading on
    As at a kingly throne,
    To lay their gold and odours sweet
    Before Thy infant feet.

The earth and ocean were not hush'd to hear
Bright harmony from every starry sphere;
Nor at Thy presence broke the voice of song
    From all the cherub choirs
    And seraph's burning lyres
Pour'd through the host of Heaven the charmèd
    clouds along.
    One angel troop the strain began,
    Of all the race of man
    By simple shepherds heard alone,
    That soft Hosanna tone.
H. H. Milman

XXXI

GOD INCARNATE

    The Holy Son of God most high,
        For love of Adam's lapsèd race,
    Quit the sweet pleasure of the sky,
        To bring us to that happy place.

    His robes of light He laid aside,
        Which did His Majesty adorn,
    And the frail state of mortal tried,
        In human flesh and figure born.

    The Son of God thus man became,
        That men the son of God might be,
    And by their second birth regain
        A likeness to His deity.
Henry Moore

XXXII
AN HYMN ON THE NATIVITY OF MY SAVIOUR

I sing the birth was born to night,
The Author both of life and light;
    The angels so did sound it.
And like the ravish'd shepherds said
Who saw the light, and were afraid,
    Yet search'd, and true they found it.

The Son of God, th' Eternal King,
That did us all salvation bring,
    And freed the soul from danger;
He whom the whole world could not take,
The Word which heaven and earth did make,
    Was now laid in a manger.

The Father's wisdom will'd it so,
The Son's obedience knew no No,
    Both wills were in one stature:
And as that wisdom had decreed,
The Word was now made flesh indeed,
    And took on Him our nature.

What comfort by Him do we win,
Who made Himself the price of sin,
    To make us heirs of glory!
To see this babe all innocence,
A martyr born in our defence:
    Can man forget this story?

Ben Jonson

XXXIII
THE BIRTH OF CHRIST

The time draws near the birth of Christ:
   The moon is hid ; the night is still ;
   The Christmas bells from hill to hill
Answer each other in the mist.

Four voices of four hamlets round,
   From far and near, on mead and moor,
   Swell out and fail, as if a door
Were shut between me and the sound.

Each voice four changes on the wind,
   That now dilate, and now decrease,
   Peace and goodwill, goodwill and peace,
Peace and goodwill, to all mankind.

Rise, happy morn ! rise, holy morn !
   Draw forth the cheerful day from night :
   O Father ! touch the east, and light
The light that shone when hope was born.
                       A. Tennyson

XXXIV
HYMN TO THE NATIVITY

Gloomy night embraced the place
   Where the noble Infant lay ;
The Babe look'd up and show'd His face—
   In spite of darkness it was day.
It was Thy day, sweet, and did rise
Not from the east, but from Thy eyes,

Book of Poetry 37

We saw Thee in Thy balmy nest,
  Bright dawn of our eternal day ;
We saw Thine eyes break from the east
  And chase the trembling shades away :
We saw Thee (and we bless'd the sight),
We saw Thee by Thine own sweet light.

Welcome to our wond'ring sight,
  Eternity shut in a span !
Summer in winter ! day in night !
  Heaven in earth ! and God in man !
Great Little One, whose glorious birth
Lifts earth to heaven, stoops heaven to earth.
                                    R. Crashaw

XXXV

LINES

Suggested by a Picture of the Adoration of the Magians

Little pomp or earthly state
On the Saviour's way might wait ;
Few the homages, and small,
That the guilty earth at all
Was permitted to accord
To her King and hidden Lord.
Therefore do we set more store
On those few, and prize them more :
Dear to us for this account
Is the glory of the Mount,
When bright beams of light did spring
Thro' the sackcloth covering,

Rays of glory found their way
Thro' the garment of decay,
With which, as with a cloak, He had
His divinest splendour clad ;
Dear the precious ointment shed
On His feet, and on His head ;
And the high-raised hope sublime,
And the triumph of the time
When thro' Zion's streets the way
Of her peaceful Conqueror lay,
Who, fulfilling ancient fame,
Meek, and with salvation came.
But of all this scanty state
That upon His steps might wait,
Dearest are those Magian Kings
With their far-brought offerings.
From what region of the morn
Are ye come thus travel-worn,
With those boxes pearl-embost,
Caskets rare, and gifts of cost?
While your swarth attendants wait
At the stable's outer gate,
And the camels lift their head
High above the lowly shed ;
Or are seen a long-drawn train
Winding down into the plain,
From below the light blue line
Of the hills in distance fine.

Dear for your own sake, whence are ye ?
Dearer for the mystery
That is round you—on what skies
Gazing, saw you first arise

Thro' the darkness that clear star
Which has marshall'd you so far,
Even unto this strawy tent,
Dancing up the Orient?
Shall we name you kings indeed,
Or is this our idle creed?
Kings of Seba, with the gold
And the incense long foretold?
Would the Gentile world by you
First-fruits pay of tribute due ;
Or have Israel's scatter'd race,
From their unknown hiding-place,
Sent to claim their part and right
In the Child new-born to night?

But although we may not guess
Of your lineage, not the less
We the self-same gifts would bring
For a spiritual offering.
May the frankincense in air ,
As it climbs instruct our prayer,
That it ever upward tend,
Ever struggle to ascend,
Leaving earth, yet ere it go
Fragrance rich diffuse below.
As the myrrh is bitter sweet,
So in us may such things meet,
As unto the mortal taste
Bitter seeming, yet at last
Shall to them who try be known
To have sweetness of their own—
Tears for sin, which sweeter far
Than the world's mad laughters are ;

Desires, that in their dying give
Pain, but die that we may live.
And the gold from Araby—
Fitter symbol who could see
Of the love which, thrice refined,
Love to God and to our kind,
Duly tender'd, He will call
Best pleasing sacrifice of all?

Thus so soon as far apart
From the proud world, in our heart
As in stable dark, defiled,
There is born th' Eternal Child,
May to Him the spirit's kings
Bear their choicest offerings;
May the affections, reason, will,
Wait upon Him to fulfil
His behests, and early pay
Homage to His natal day.
Archbishop Trench

XXXVI

THE CHILDHOOD OF CHRIST

By cool Siloam's shady rill
   How sweet the lily grows;
How sweet the breath beneath the hill
   Of Sharon's dewy rose:
Lo such the child whose early feet
   The paths of peace have trod;
Whose secret heart with influence sweet
   Is lifted up to God.

By cool Siloam's shady rill
  The lily must decay;
The rose that blooms beneath the hill
  Must shortly fade away;
And soon, too soon, the wintry hour
  Of man's maturer age
Will shake the soul with sorrow's power,
  And stormy passion's rage.

O Thou whose infant feet were found
  Within Thy Father's shrine,
Whose years with changeless virtue crown'd
  Were all alike Divine:
Dependent on Thy bounteous breath,
  We seek Thy grace alone
In childhood, manhood, age, and death,
  To keep us still Thine own.
              Bishop Heber

XXXVII

GLORIES OF THE MESSIAH.

Rise, crown'd with light, imperial Salem rise,
Exalt thy towery head, and lift thy eyes!
See a long race thy spacious courts adorn;
See future sons and daughters, yet unborn,
In crowding ranks on every side arise,
Demanding life, impatient for the skies!
See barbarous nations at thy gate attend,
Walk in thy light, and in thy temple bend;
See thy bright altars throng'd with prostrate kings,
And heap'd with products of Sabean springs!
For thee, Idume's spicy forests blow,
And seeds of gold in Ophir's mountains glow.

See Heaven its sparkling portals wide display,
And break upon thee in a flood of day.
No more the rising sun shall gild the morn,
Nor evening Cynthia fill her silver horn;
But lost, dissolved in thy superior rays,
One tide of glory, one unclouded blaze
O'erflow thy courts: the Light Himself shall shine
Reveal'd, and God's eternal day be thine!
The seas shall waste, the skies in smoke decay,
Rocks fall to dust, and mountains melt away;
But fixed His word, His saving power remains;
Thy realm for ever lasts, thy own Messiah reigns.
A. Pope

XXXVIII
CHRIST BETRAYED

Eighteen hundred years agone
Was that deed of darkness done—
Was that sacred thorn-crown'd head
To a shameful death betray'd,
And Iscariot's traitor name
Blazon'd in eternal shame.
Thou, disciple of our time,
Follower of the faith sublime,
Who with high and holy scorn
Of that traitorous deed dost burn,
Though the years may nevermore
To our earth that form restore,
The Christ-spirit ever lives—
Ever in thy heart He strives.
When pale misery mutely calls,
When thy brother tempted falls,
When thy gentle words may chain

Hate, and anger, and disdain,
Or thy loving smile impart
Courage to some sinking heart:
When within thy troubled breast
Good and evil thoughts contest,
Though unconscious thou mayst be,
The Christ-spirit strives with thee.

   When He trod the holy land
With His small disciple band,
And the fated hour had come
For that august martyrdom—
When the man, the human love,
And the God within Him strove—
As in Gethsemane He wept,
They, the faithless watchers, slept:
While for them He wept and pray'd,
One denied and one betray'd!

   If to-day thou turn'st aside
In thy luxury and pride,
Wrapp'd within thyself, and blind
To the sorrows of thy kind,
Thou a faithless watch dost keep—
Thou art one of those who sleep:
Or, if waking, thou dost see
Nothing of divinity
In our fallen struggling race—
If in them thou see'st no trace
Of a glory dimmed, not gone,
Of a future to be won,
Of a future, hopeful, high,
Thou, like Peter, dost deny:

The Sunday

    But, if seeing, thou believest,
    If the Evangel thou receivest,
    Yet, if thou art bound to sin,
    False to the ideal within,
    Slave of ease, or slave of gold,
    Thou the Son of God hast sold.
A. C. Lynch

XXXIX

THE DEATH OF CHRIST

Lord Jesu, when we stand afar
    And gaze upon Thy Holy Cross,
In love of Thee and scorn of self,
    O, may we count the world as loss!

When we behold Thy bleeding wounds,
    And the rough way that Thou hast trod,
Make us to hate the load of sin
    That lay so heavy on our God.

O holy Lord! uplifted high
    With outstretch'd arms, in mortal woe,
Embracing in Thy wondrous love
    The sinful world that lies below:

Give us an ever living faith
    To gaze beyond the things we see;
And in the mystery of Thy Death
    Draw us and all men unto Thee!
William Walsham Howe

XL
GOOD FRIDAY

Bound upon th' accursèd tree,
Faint and bleeding, who is He?
By the eyes so pale and dim,
Streaming blood and writhing limb,
By the flesh with scourges torn,
By the crown of twisted thorn,
By the side so deeply pierced,
By the baffled burning thirst,
By the drooping death-dew'd brow,
Son of Man! 'tis Thou! 'tis Thou!

Bound upon th' accursèd tree,
Dread and awful, who is He?
By the sun at noonday pale,
Shivering rocks, and rending veil,
By earth that trembles at His doom,
By yonder saints, who burst their tomb,
By Eden promised, ere He died,
To the felon at His side;
Lord, our suppliant knees we bow,
Son of God! 'tis Thou! 'tis Thou!

Bound upon th' accursèd tree,
Sad, and dying, who is He?
By the last and bitter cry,
The ghost given up in agony,
By the lifeless body laid
In the chamber of the dead,

By the mourners come to weep
Where the bones of Jesus sleep;
Crucified! we know Thee now;
Son of Man! 'tis Thou! 'tis Thou!

Bound upon th' accursèd tree,
Dread and awful, who is He?
By the prayer for them that slew—
" Lord! they know not what they do!"
By the spoil'd and empty grave,
By the souls He died to save,
By the conquest He hath won,
By the saints before His throne,
By the rainbow round His brow,
Son of God! 'tis Thou! 'tis Thou!

Henry Hart Milman

XLI
"*THEY CRUCIFIED HIM*"

O come and mourn with me awhile;
O come ye to the Saviour's side;
O come, together let us mourn:
Jesus, our Lord, is crucified.

Have we no tears to shed for Him
While soldiers scoff, and Jews deride?
Ah, look how patiently He hangs;
Jesus, our Lord, is crucified.

How fast His hands and feet are nail'd;
His throat with parching thirst is dried;
His failing eyes are dimm'd with blood;
Jesus, our Lord, is crucified.

Seven times He spake, seven words of love;
And all three hours His silence cried
For mercy on the souls of men;
Jesus, our Lord, is crucified.

Come, let us stand beneath the cross;
So may the blood from out His side
Fall gently on us, drop by drop;
Jesus, our Lord, is crucified.

A broken heart, a fount of tears,
Ask, and they will not be denied;
Lord Jesus, may we love, and weep,
Since Thou for us art crucified.
     Frederic W. Faber

XLII

LITANY TO THE SAVIOUR

When our heads are bow'd with woe,
When our bitter tears o'erflow,
When we mourn the lost, the dear,
Gracious Son of Mary, hear!

Thou our throbbing flesh hast worn
Thou our mortal griefs hast borne,
Thou hast shed the human tear,
Gracious Son of Mary, hear!

When the sullen death-bell tolls
For our own departing souls;
When our final doom is near,
Gracious Son of Mary, hear!

Thou hast bow'd the dying head ;
Thou the blood of life hast shed ;
Thou hast fill'd a mortal bier :
Gracious Son of Mary, hear !

When the heart is sad within
With the thought of all its sin,
When the spirit shrinks with fear,
Gracious Son of Mary, hear !

Thou the shame, the grief hast known,
Though the sins were not Thine own ;
Thou hast deign'd their load to bear,
Gracious Son of Mary, hear !
Henry Hart Milman

XLIII

LITANY TO OUR LORD

Saviour, when in dust to Thee
Low we bow th' adoring knee ;
When repentant to the skies
Scarce we lift our weeping eyes ;
O, by all Thy pain and woe
Suffer'd once for man below,
Bending from Thy throne on high,
Hear our solemn Litany !

By Thy helpless infant years,
By Thy life of want and tears,
By Thy days of sore distress
In the savage wilderness,

By the dread mysterious hour
Of the insulting tempter's power,
Turn, O turn a favouring eye ;
Hear our solemn Litany !

By the sacred griefs that wept
O'er the grave where Lazarus slept ;
By the boding tears that flow'd
Over Salem's lov'd abode ;
By the anguish'd sigh that told
Treachery lurk'd within Thy fold ;
From Thy seat above the sky,
Hear our solemn Litany !

By Thine hour of dire despair,
By Thine agony of prayer,
By the cross, the nail, the thorn,
Piercing spear, and torturing scorn ;
By the gloom that veil'd the skies
O'er the dreadful sacrifice ;
Listen to our humble cry,
Hear our solemn Litany !

By Thy deep expiring groan ;
By the sad sepulchral stone ;
By the vault, whose dark abode
Held in vain the rising God ;
O ! from earth to heaven restored,
Mighty re-ascended Lord,
Listen, listen to the cry
Of our solemn Litany.

Sir R. Grant

XLIV

TO THE SAVIOUR

Star of morn and even,
Sun of Heaven's heaven,
  Saviour high and dear
  Toward us turn Thine ear;
  Through whate'er may come,
  Thou canst lead us home.

Though the gloom be grievous,
Those we leant on leave us,
  Though the coward heart
  Quit its proper part,
  Though the Tempter come,
  Thou wilt lead us home.

Saviour pure and holy,
Lover of the lowly,
  Sign us with Thy sign,
  Take our hands in Thine,
  Take our hands and come,
  Lead Thy children home.

Star of morn and even,
Shine on us from Heaven,
  From Thy glory-throne
  Hear Thy very own!
  Lord and Saviour, come,
  Lead us to our home!

F. T. Palgrave

XLV

THE CROSS

When I survey the wondrous cross
  On which the Prince of Glory died,
My richest gain I count but loss,
  And pour contempt on all my pride.

Forbid it, Lord, that I should boast,
  Save in the death of Christ, my God;
All the vain things that charm me most,
  I sacrifice them to His blood.

See from His head, His hands, His feet,
  Sorrow and love flow mingled down!
Did e'er such love and sorrow meet,
  Or thorns compose so rich a crown?

Were the whole realm of nature mine,
  That were a present far too small;
Love so amazing, so divine,
  Demands my soul, my life, my all.
              Isaac Watts

XLVI

ROCK OF AGES

Rock of Ages, cleft for me,
Let me hide myself in Thee!
Let the water and the blood,
From Thy riven side which flow'd,
Be of sin the double cure,
Cleanse me from its guilt and power.

Not the labours of my hands
Can fulfil Thy law's demands ;
Could my zeal no respite know,
Could my tears for ever flow,
All for sin could not atone ;
Thou must save, and Thou alone.

Nothing in my hand I bring ;
Simply to Thy cross I cling ;
Naked, come to Thee for dress ;
Helpless, look to Thee for grace ;
Foul, I to the Fountain fly ;
Wash me, Saviour, or I die !

While I draw this fleeting breath
When my heartstrings break in death,
When I soar through tracts unknown,
See Thee on Thy judgment-throne ;
Rock of Ages, cleft for me,
Let me hide myself in Thee !

A. M. Toplady

XLVII

HYMN FOR EASTER EVE

All is o'er ;—the pain—the sorrow—
 Human taunts, and fiendish spite,
Death shall be despoil'd to-morrow
 Of the prey he grasps to-night ;
Yet, once more to seal His doom,
Christ must sleep within the tomb.

Close and still the cell that holds Him,
    While in brief repose He lies ;
Deep the slumber that enfolds Him,
    Veil'd awhile from mortal eyes :—
Slumber, such as needs must be
After hard-won victory.

Fierce and deadly was the anguish
    Which on yonder cross He bore ;
How did soul and body languish,
    Till the toil of death was o'er !
But that toil, so fierce and dread,
Bruis'd and crush'd the serpent's head.

Whither hath His soul departed ?—
    Roams it on some blissful shore,
Where the meek and faithful-hearted,
    Vext by this world's hate no more,
Wait until the trump of doom
Call their bodies from the tomb?

Or, on some benignant mission,
    To the imprison'd spirits sent,
Hath He to their dark condition
    Gleams of hope and mercy lent?
Souls not wholly lost of old
When o'er earth the deluge roll'd !

Ask no more ;—the abyss is deeper
    E'en than angels' thoughts may scan :
Come and watch the Heavenly Sleeper ;
    Come, and do what mortals can,
Reverence meet toward Him to prove,
Faith, and trust, and humble love.

Far away, amidst the regions
  Of the bright and balmy east,
Guarded by angelic legions,
  Till death's slumber shall have ceased,
(How should we its stillness stir?)
Lies the Saviour's sepulchre.

Far away;—yet thought would wander
  (Thought by faith's sure guidance led)
Farther yet to weep, and ponder
  Over that sepulchral bed.
Thither let us haste, and flee
On the wings of phantasy.

Haste, from every clime and nation,
  Fervent youth, and rev'rent age;
Peasant, prince,—each rank and station,—
  Haste, and join this pilgrimage.
East and west, and south and north,
Send your saintliest spirits forth.

Mothers, ere the curtain closes
  Round your children's sleep to-night,
Tell them how their Lord reposes,
  Waiting for to-morrow's light;
Teach their dreams to Him to rove,
Him who lov'd them, Him they love.

Matron grave and blooming maiden,
  Hoary sage and beardless boy,
Hearts with grief and care o'erladen,
  Hearts brimful of hope and joy,
Come, and greet in death's dark hall,
Him who felt with, felt for all.

Men of God, devoutly toiling
   This world's fetters to unbind ;
Satan of his prey despoiling
   In the hearts of human kind ;
Let, to-night, your labours cease,
Give your care-worn spirits peace.

Ye who roam our seas and mountains,
   Messengers of love and light ;
Ye who guard truth's sacred fountains,
   Weary day and wakeful night ;
Men of labour, men of lore,
Give your toils and studies o'er.

Dwellers in the woods and valleys,
   Ye of meek and lowly breast ;
Ye who, pent in crowded alleys,
   Labour early, late take rest ;
Leave the plough, and leave the loom ;
Meet us at our Saviour's tomb.

From your halls of stately beauty,
   Sculptur'd roof, and marble floor,
In this work of Christian duty
   Haste, ye rich, and join the poor.
Mean and noble, bond and free
Meet in frank equality.

Lo, His grave ! the grey rock closes
   O'er that virgin burial-ground ;
Near it breathe the garden roses,
   Trees funereal droop around,
In whose boughs the small birds rest,
And the stock-dove builds her nest.

And the morn with floods of splendour
    Fills the spicy midnight air;
Tranquil sounds, and voices tender,
    Speak of life and gladness there;
Ne'er was living thing, I wot,
Which our Lord regarded not.

Bird, and beast, and insect rover,—
    E'en the lilies of the field,
Till His gentle life was over,
    Heavenly thought to Him could yield.
All that is, to Him did prove,
Food for wisdom, food for love.

But the hearts that bow'd before Him
    Most of all to Him were dear;
Let such hearts to-night watch o'er Him
    Till the day-spring shall appear:—
Then a brighter sun shall rise
Than e'er kindled up the skies.

All night long, with plaintive voicing,
    Chant His requiem soft and low;
Loftier strains of loud rejoicing
    From to-morrow's harps shall flow.
" Death and hell at length are slain,
Christ hath triumph'd, Christ doth reign."

J. Moultrie

XLVIII
THE RESURRECTION

I got me flowers to strew Thy way;
I got me boughs off many a tree:
But Thou wast up by break of day
And brought'st Thy sweets along with Thee.

The sun arising in the East,
'Though he give light, and the East perfume ;
If they should offer to contest
With Thy arising, they presume.

Can there be any day but this,
Though many suns to shine endeavour?
We count three hundred, but we miss :
There is but One, and that One ever.
George Herbert

XLIX
THE ASCENSION
He is gone—beyond the skies,
A cloud receives Him from our eyes ;
Gone beyond the highest height
Of mortal gaze or angel's flight ;
Through the veils of time and space,
Pass'd into the holiest place ;
All the toil, the sorrow done,
All the battle fought and won.

He is gone—and we return,
And our hearts within us burn ;
Olivet no more shall greet,
With welcome shout, His coming feet ;
Never shall we track Him more
On Gennesareth's glist'ning shore,
Never in that look, or voice,
Shall Zion's walls again rejoice.

He is gone—and we remain
In this world of sin and pain,
In the void which He has left ;
On this earth, of Him bereft ;

We have still His work to do,
We can still His path pursue,
Seek Him both in friend or foe,
In ourselves His image show.

He is gone—but we once more
Shall behold Him as before,
In the Heaven of Heavens, the same
As on earth He went and came;
In the many mansions there,
Peace for us He will prepare,
In that world unseen, unknown,
He and we may yet be one.

He is gone—but not in vain;
Wait, until He comes again;
He is risen, He is not here,
Far above this earthly sphere;
Evermore in heart, and mind,
There our peace in Him we find,
To our own Eternal Friend,
Thitherward let us ascend.
A. P. Stanley

L

CHRIST'S ASCENSION

God is ascended up on high,
  With merry noise of trumpet-sound,
And princely seated in the sky,
  Rules over all the world around.

Sing praises then, sing praises loud
  Unto our universal King:
He who ascended on a cloud,
  To Him all laud and praises sing.

In human flesh and shape He went,
    Adornèd with His passion's scars ;
Which in Heaven's sight He did present
    More glorious than the glittering stars.

O happy pledge of pardon sure,
    And of an endless blissful state,
Since human nature once made pure,
    For Heaven becomes so fit a mate !

Lord, raise our sinking minds therefore,
    Up to our proper country dear ;
And purify us evermore,
    To fit us for those regions clear.

That when He shall return again
    In clouds of glory, as He went,
Our souls no foulness may retain,
    But be found pure and innocent.

And so may mount to His bright hosts
    On eagle wings up to the sky,
And be conducted to the courts
    Of everlasting bliss and joy.
                  Henry Moore

LI

CHRIST OUR GOD

He, Who on earth as man was known,
    And bore our sins and pains,
Now, seated on the eternal Throne,
    The God of Glory reigns.

His hands the wheels of Nature guide
   With an unerring skill,
And countless worlds, extended wide,
   Obey His sovereign will.

While harps unnumber'd sound His praise
   In yonder world above,
His saints on earth admire His ways
   And glory in His love.

His righteousness, to faith reveal'd,
   Wrought out for guilty worms,
Affords a hiding-place and shield
   From enemies and storms.

This land through which His pilgrims go,
   Is desolate and dry;
But streams of grace from Him o'erflow,
   Their thirst to satisfy.

When troubles, like a burning sun,
   Beat heavy on their head,
To this Almighty Rock they run,
   And find a pleasing shade.

How glorious He! how happy they
   In such a glorious Friend!
Whose love secures them all the way,
   And crowns them at the end.

J. Newton

LII
THE MEDIATOR

Where high the heavenly temple stands,
The house of God not made with hands,
A great High Priest our nature wears,
The Saviour of mankind appears.

He who for man in mercy stood,
And pour'd on earth His precious blood,
Pursues in heaven His plan of grace,
The guardian God of human race.

Though now ascended up on high,
He bends on earth a brother's eye,
Partaker of the human name,
He knows the frailty of our frame.

Our fellow-sufferer yet retains
A fellow-feeling for our pains ;
And still remembers, in the skies,
His tears, and agonies, and cries.

In every pang that rends the heart
The Man of Sorrows had a part ;
He sympathises in our grief,
And to the sufferer sends relief.

With boldness, therefore, at the throne,
Let us make all our sorrows known,
And ask the aids of heavenly power,
To help us in the evil hour.

J. Logan

III

THE WRITTEN WORD

LIII

THE BIBLE

Dim—as the borrow'd beams of moon and stars
To lonely, weary, wandering travellers—
Is reason to the soul: and as on high,
Those rolling fires discover but the sky,
Not light us here; so reason's glimmering ray
Was lent, not to assure our doubtful way,
But guide us upward to a better day.
And as those nightly tapers disappear
When day's bright lord ascends our hemisphere,
So pale grows Reason at Religion's sight;
So dies, and so dissolves in supernatural light.
John Dryden

LIV

THE GOSPELS

And so the Word had breath, and wrought
  With human hands, the creed of creeds
  In loveliness of perfect deeds,
More strong than all poetic thought.

Which he may read that binds the sheaf,
  Or builds the house, or digs the grave,
  And those wild eyes that watch the wave
In roarings round the coral reef.
A. Tennyson

LV
THE SECOND DAY OF CREATION

This world I deem
But a beautiful dream
Of shadows that are not what they seem,
Where visions rise,
Giving dim surmise
Of the things that shall meet our waking eyes.

Arm of the Lord !
Creating Word !
Whose glory the silent skies record
Where stands Thy name
In scrolls of flame
On the firmament's high-shadowing frame.

I gaze o'erhead,
Where Thy hand hath spread
For the waters of Heaven that crystal bed,
And stored the dew
In its deeps of blue,
Which the fires of the sun come temper'd through.

Soft they shine
Through that pure shrine,
As beneath the veil of Thy flesh divine,
Beams forth the light
That were else too bright
For the feebleness of a sinner's sight.

I gaze aloof
On the tissued roof,
Where time and space are the warp and woof,

      Which the King of kings
      As a curtain flings
O'er the dreadfulness of eternal things—

      A tapestried tent
      To shade us meant
From the bare everlasting firmament ;
      Where the blaze of the skies
      Comes soft to our eyes
Through a veil of mystical imageries.

      But could I see
      As in truth they be,
The glories of Heaven that encompass me,
      I should lightly hold
      The tissued fold
Of that marvellous curtain of blue and gold.

      Soon the whole
      Like a parchèd scroll
Shall before my amazèd sight uproll,
      And without a screen
      At one burst be seen
The Presence wherein I have ever been.

      O ! who shall bear
      The blinding glare
Of the Majesty that shall meet us there ?
      What eye may gaze
      On the unveil'd blaze
Of the light-girdled throne of the Ancient of days ?
      Christ us aid !
      Himself be our shade,
That in that dread day we be not dismay'd.
                      T. Whytehead

LVI

THE THIRD DAY OF CREATION

Thou spakest, and the waters roll'd
  Back from the earth away,
They fled, by Thy strong voice controll'd,
  Till Thou didst bid them stay:
Then did that rushing, mighty ocean,
Like a tame creature cease its motion,
Nor dared to pass where'er Thy hand
Had fix'd its bound of slender sand.

And freshly risen from out the deep
  The land lay tranquil now
Like a new-christen'd child asleep
  With the dew upon its brow:
As when in after time the earth
Rose from her second watery birth,
In pure baptismal garments drest,
And calmly waiting to be blest.

Again Thou spakest, Lord of power,
  And straight the land was seen
All clad with tree, and herb, and flower,
  A robe of lustrous green:
Like souls, wherein the hidden strength
Of their new birth is waked at length,
When, robed in holiness, they tell
What might did in those waters dwell.

F

Lord, o'er the waters of my soul
  The word of peace be said;
Its thoughts and passions bid Thou roll
  Each in its channell'd bed;
Till that in peaceful order flowing,
They time their glad obedient going
To Thy commands, whose voice to-day
Bade the tumultuous floods obey.

For, restless as the moaning sea,
  The wild and wayward will
From side to side is wearily
  Changing and tossing still;
But sway'd by Thee, 'tis like the river
That down its green banks flows for ever,
And calm, and constant tells to all
The blessedness of such sweet thrall.

Then in my heart, Spirit of might,
  Awake the life within
And bid a spring-tide, calm and bright,
  Of holiness begin:
So let it lie with Heaven's grace
Full shining on its quiet face,
Like the young earth in peace profound,
Amid the assuagèd waters round.

T. Whytchead

LVII

THE SEVENTH DAY OF CREATION

Sabbath of the saints of old,
Day of mysteries manifold;
By the great Creator blest,
Type of His eternal rest:

I with thoughts of thee would seek
To sanctify the closing week.

Resting from His work, the Lord
Spake to-day the hallowing word;
And, His wondrous labours done,
Now the everlasting Son
Gave to heaven and earth the sign
Of a wonder more divine.

Resting from His work to-day,
In the tomb the Saviour lay,
His sacred form from head to feet
Swathèd in the winding sheet,
Lying in the rock alone,
Hid beneath the sealèd stone.

All the seventh day long I ween
Mournful watch'd the Magdalene,
Rising early, resting late,
By the sepulchre to wait,
In the holy garden glade
Where her buried Lord was laid.

So with Thee till life shall end
I would solemn vigil spend;
Let me hew Thee, Lord, a shrine
In this rocky heart of mine,
Where in pure embalmèd cell
None but Thou may'st ever dwell.

Myrrh and spices I will bring,
My poor affection's offering,

Close the door from sight and sound
Of the busy world around,
And in patient watch remain
Till my Lord appear again.

Then, the new creation done,
Shall be Thy endless rest begun;
Jesu, keep me safe from sin,
That I with them may enter in,
And danger past, and toil at end,
To Thy resting place ascend.

T. Whytehead

LVIII

SLEEPING ON THE WATERS

While snows, even from the mild south-west,
   Come blinding o'er all day,
What kindlier home, what safer nest
   For flower or fragrant spray,
Than underneath some cottage roof,
   Where fires are bright within,
And fretting cares scowl far aloof,
   And doors are closed on sin?

The scarlet tufts so cheerily
   Look out upon the snow,
But gayer smiles the maiden eye
   Whose garden care they know.
The buds that in that nook are born,
   Through the dark howling day
Old winter's spite they laugh to scorn:—
   Who is so safe as they?

Nay, look again, beside the hearth
   The lowly cradle mark,
Where weary with his ten hours' mirth
   Sleeps in his own warm ark
A bright-haired babe, with arm uprais'd
   As though the slumberous dew
Stole o'er him, while in faith he gazed
   Upon his guardian true.

Storms may rush in, and crimes and woes
   Deform the quiet bower ;
They may not mar the deep repose
   Of that immortal flower.
Though only broken hearts be found
   To watch his cradle by,
No blight is on his slumbers sound,
   No touch of harmful eye.

So gently slumber'd on the wave
   The new-born seer of old,
Ordained the chosen tribes to save ;
   Nor deem'd how darkly roll'd
The waters by his rushy bark,
   Perchance e'en now defiled
With infant's blood for Israel's sake,
   Blood of some priestly child.

What recks he of his mother's tears,
   His sister's boding sigh ?
The whispering reeds are all he hears,
   And Nile, soft weltering nigh,
Sings him to sleep, but he will wake,
   And o'er the haughty flood
Wave his stern rod ; and lo ! a lake,
   A restless sea of blood !

Soon shall a mightier flood thy call
  And outstretch'd rod obey;
To right and left the watery wall
  From Israel shrinks away.
Such honour wins the faith that gave
  Thee, and thy sweetest boon
Of infant charms to the rude wave,
  In the third joyous moon.

Hail, chosen type and image true
  Of Jesus on the sea!
In slumber and in glory too
  Shadow'd of old by Thee—
Save that in calmness thou didst sleep
  The summer stream beside;
He on a wider wilder deep,
  Where boding night-winds sigh'd.

Sigh'd when at eve He laid Him down,
  But with a sound like flame
At midnight from the mountain's crown
  Upon His slumbers came.
Lo, how they watch, till He awake,
  Around His rude low bed;
How wistful count the waves that break
  So near His sacred head.

O, faithless! know ye not of old
  How in the western bay,
When dark and vast the billows roll'd,
  A prophet slumbering lay?
The surges smote the keel as fast
  As thunderbolts from heaven,
Himself into the wave he cast,
  And hope and life were given.

Behold a mightier far is here;
   Nor will He spare to leap,
For the soul's sake He loves so dear,
   Into a wilder deep.
E'en now He dreams of Calvary;
   Soon will He wake, and say
The words of peace and might: Do ye
   His hour in calmness stay.
                              J. Keble

LIX

THE DESTROYING ANGEL

      He stopp'd at last
And a mild look of sacred pity cast
Down on the sinful land where he was sent
T' inflict the tardy punishment.

"Ah! yet," said he, "yet, stubborn king, repent,
   Whilst thus unarm'd I stand,
Ere the keen sword of God fill my commanded
      hand;
Suffer but yet thyself and thine to live:
   Who would, alas! believe
   That it for man," said he,
" So hard to be forgiven should be,
And yet for God so easy to forgive!"

Through Egypt's wicked land his march he took,
And as he march'd the sacred firstborn strook
   Of every womb: none did he spare,
None, from the meanest beast to Pharaoh's purple
      heir.

Whilst health and strength and gladness doth
    possess
  The festal Hebrew cottages;
The blest destroyer comes not there
To interrupt the sacred cheer:
Upon their doors he read, and understood
  God's protection writ in blood;
Well was he skill'd i' the character divine;
  And though he pass'd by it in haste,
  He bow'd and worshipp'd, as he pass'd,
The mighty mystery through its humble sign.

A. Cowley

LX

HOPES IN THE WILDERNESS

From the song of the Manna Gatherers

We beside the wondrous river
  In the appointed hour shall stand,
Following, as from Egypt ever,
  Thy bright cloud, and outstretch'd hand:
    In thy shadow,
  We shall rest on Abraham's land.

Not by manna showers at morning
  Shall our board be then supplied,
But a strange pale gold adorning
  Many a tufted mountain side,
    Yearly feed us,
  Year by year our murmurings chide.

There, no prophet's touch awaiting,
  From each cool deep cavern start
Rills, that since their first creating
  Ne'er have ceased to play their part.
    Oft we hear them
  In our dreams with thirsty heart.

Deeps of blessing are before us :
  Only while the desert sky
And the sheltering cloud hang o'er us
  Morn by morn obediently,
    Glean we manna,
  And the song of Moses try.
                    J. Keble

LXI

THE BURIAL OF MOSES

By Nebo's lonely mountain,
  On this side Jordan's wave,
In a vale in the land of Moab
  There lies a lonely grave.
And no man knows that sepulchre,
  And no man saw it e'er,
For the angels of God upturned the sod,
  And laid the dead man there.

That was the grandest funeral
  That ever passed on earth ;
But no man heard the trampling,
  Or saw the train go forth—
Noiselessly as the daylight
  Comes back when night is done,
And the crimson streak on ocean's cheek
  Grows into the great sun.

Noiselessly as the spring time
    Her crown of verdure weaves,
And all the trees on all the hills
    Open their thousand leaves;
So without sound of music,
    Or voice of them that wept,
Silently down from the mountain's crown,
    The great procession swept.

Perchance the bald old eagle,
    On grey Beth-Peor's height,
Out of his lonely eyrie,
    Look'd on the wondrous sight;
Perchance the lion stalking
    Still shuns that hallow'd spot,
For beast and bird have seen and heard
    That which man knoweth not.

But when the warrior dieth,
    His comrades in the war,
With arms reversed and muffled drum,
    Follow his funeral car;
They show the banners taken,
    They tell his battles won,
And after him lead his masterless steed,
    While peals the minute gun.

Amid the noblest of the land
    We lay the sage to rest,
And give the bard an honour'd place,
    With costly marble drest,
In the great minster transept
    Where lights like glories fall,
And the organ rings, and the sweet choir sings
    Along the emblazoned wall.

This was the truest warrior
  That ever buckled sword,
This the most gifted poet
  That ever breath'd a word;
And never earth's philosopher
  Traced with his golden pen,
On the deathless page, truths half so sage
  As he wrote down for men.

And had he not high honour,—
  The hill-side for a pall,
To lie in state while angels wait
  With stars for tapers tall,
And the dark rock-pines, like tossing plumes,
  Over his bier to wave,
And God's own hand in that lonely land,
  To lay him in the grave?

In that strange grave without a name,
  Whence his uncoffin'd clay
Shall break again, O wondrous thought!
  Before the Judgment day,
And stand with glory wrapt around
  On the hills he never trod,
And speak of the strife that won our life,
  With the Incarnate Son of God.

O lonely grave in Moab's land!
  O dark Beth-Peor's hill!
Speak to these curious hearts of ours,
  And teach them to be still.
God hath His mysteries of grace,
  Ways that we cannot tell;
He hides them deep, like the hidden sleep
  Of him He loved so well.

                  C. F. Alexander

LXII

THE CALL OF DAVID

Latest born of Jesse's race,
Wonder lights thy bashful face,
While the prophet's gifted oil
Seals thee for a path of toil.
We, thy angels circling round thee
Ne'er shall find thee as we found thee,
When thy faith first brought us near,
In thy lion fight severe.

Go! and 'mid thy flocks awhile
At thy doom of greatness smile;
Bold to bear God's heaviest load,
Dimly guessing of the road—
Rocky road, and scarce ascended
Though thy foot be angel-tended!
Double praise thou shalt attain
In royal court, and battle plain:
Then comes heart-ache, care, distress,
Blighted hope, and loneliness,
Wounds from friend, and gifts from foe,
Dizzied faith, and guilt, and woe,
Loftiest aims by earth defiled,
Gleams of wisdom, sin-beguil'd,
Sated power's tyrannic mood,
Counsels shared with men of blood.

Strange that guileless face and form,
To lavish on the scarring storm!
Yet we take thee in thy blindness,
And we harass thee in kindness;

Little chary of thy fame—
Dust unborn may bless or blame—
But we mould thee for the root
Of man's promised healing fruit,
And we mould thee hence to rise
As our brother in the skies.
J. H. Newman

LXIII

"*SOLOMON IN ALL HIS GLORY WAS NOT ARRAYED LIKE ONE OF THESE*"

When the great Hebrew king did almost strain
The wondrous treasures of his wealth and brain,
His royal southern guest to entertain;
   Though she on silver floors did tread,
With bright Assyrian carpets on them spread,
   To hide the metal's poverty;
'Though she look'd up to roofs of gold,
And nought around her could behold
   But silk and rich embroidery,
   And Babylonish tapestry,
   And wealthy Hiram's princely dye;
Though Ophir's starry stones met everywhere her eye;
Though she herself, and her gay host were drest
With all the shining glories of the East;
When lavish art her costly work had done,
   The honour and the prize of bravery
   Was by the garden from the palace won;
And every rose and lily there did stand
   Better attired by nature's hand.

Where does the wisdom and the power divine
In a more bright and sweet reflection shine?
Where do we finer strokes and colours see
Of the Creator's real poetry,
  Than when we with attention look
  Upon the third day's volume of the book?
But we despise these His inferior ways,
Though no less full of miracle and praise:
  Upon the flowers of heaven we gaze;
The stars of earth no wonder in us raise.
A. Cowley

LXIV

NAAMAN'S SERVANT

"Who for the like of me will care?"
  So whispers many a mournful heart,
When in the weary languid air,
  For grief or scorn we pine apart.

So haply mused yon little maid,
  From Israel's breezy mountain borne,
No more to rest in Sabbath shade,
  Watching the free and waving corn.

A captive now, and sold, and bought,
  In the proud Syrian's hall she waits,
Forgotten—such her moody thought—
  Even as the worm beneath the gates.

But One who ne'er forgets is here:
  He hath a word for thee to speak:
O serve Him yet in duteous fear,
  And to thy Gentile lord be meek.

So shall the healing Name be known
    By thee on many a heathen shore,
And Naaman on his chariot throne
    Wait humbly by Elisha's door.

By thee desponding lepers know
    The sacred water's sevenfold might,
Then wherefore sink in listless woe?
    Christ's poor and needy claim your right.

Your heavenly right to do and bear
    All for His sake; nor yield one sigh
To pining doubt; nor ask "What care
    In the wide world for such as I?"

                      J. Keble

LXV

THE DESTRUCTION OF THE ASSYRIANS

The Assyrian came down like the wolf on the fold,
And his cohorts were gleaming in purple and gold,
And the sheen of their spears was like stars on the sea,
When the blue wave rolls nightly on deep Galilee.

Like the leaves of the forest when summer is green,
That host with their banners at sunset were seen,
Like the leaves of the forest when autumn hath blown,
That host on the morrow lay wither'd and strown.

For the angel of death spread his wings on the blast,
And breathed on the face of the foe as he pass'd,
And the eyes of the sleeper waxed deadly and chill,
And their hearts but once heaved, and for ever grew still.

And there lay the steed with his nostril all wide,
But through it there roll'd not the breath of his pride;
And the foam of his gasping lay white on the turf,
And cold as the spray of the rock-beating surf.

And there lay the rider distorted and pale,
With the dew on his brow, and the rust on his mail;
And the tents were all silent, the banners alone,
The lances unlifted, the trumpets unblown.

And the widows of Ashur are loud in their wail,
And the idols are broke in the temple of Baal;
And the might of the Gentile, unsmote by the sword,
Hath melted like snow in the glance of the Lord.

Lord Byron

LXVI

HEAVENLY WISDOM

O, happy is the man who hears
    Instruction's warning voice,
And who celestial wisdom makes
    His early, only choice.

For she has treasures, greater far
    Than east or west unfold,
And her reward is more secure
    Than is the gain of gold.

In her right hand, she holds to view
  A length of happy years;
And in her left, the prize of fame,
  And honour bright appears.

She guides the young with innocence,
  In pleasure's path to tread;
A crown of glory she bestows
  Upon the hoary head.

According as her labours rise,
  So her rewards increase;
Her ways are ways of pleasantness,
  And all her paths are peace.
                    J. Logan

LXVII

HABAKKUK'S PRAYER

Chap. III. 17, 18.

Yet though the fig-tree should no burden bear,
Though vines delude the promise of the year;
Yet though the olive should not yield her oil,
Nor the parch'd glebe reward the peasant's toil;
Though the tired ox beneath his labours fall,
And herds in millions perish from the stall!
  Yet shall my grateful strings
  For ever praise Thy name,
  For ever Thee proclaim
The everlasting God, the mighty King of Kings.
                              Broome

LXVIII
JOB'S CONFESSION

Thou canst accomplish all things, Lord of might :
And every thought is naked to Thy sight.
But O, Thy ways are wonderful, and lie
Beyond the deepest reach of mortal eye.
Oft have I heard of Thine Almighty power,
But never saw Thee till this dreadful hour.
O'erwhelm'd with shame, the Lord of life I see,
Abhor myself, and give my soul to Thee.
Nor shall my weakness tempt Thine anger more ;
Man is not made to question, but adore.
E. Young

LXIX
THE WATERS OF BABYLON

But on before me swept the moonlit stream
That had entranced me with his memories,
A thousand battles, and one burst of Psalms—
Rolling his waters to the Indian sea
Beyond Balsara, and Elana far,
Nigh to two thousand miles from Ararat.
And his full music took a finer tone,
And sang me something of a gentler stream
That rolls for ever to another shore,
Whereof our God Himself is the sole sea,
And Christ's dear love the pulsing of the tide,
And His sweet Spirit is the breathing wind.
Something it chanted, too, of exiled men,
On the sad bank of that strange river, Life,
Hanging the harp of their deep heart-desires

To rest upon the willow of the Cross,
And longing for the everlasting hills,
Mount Sion, and Jerusalem of God.
And then I thought I knelt, and kneeling heard
Nothing—save only the long wash of waves,
And one sweet Psalm that sobb'd for evermore.
W. Alexander

LXX
THE ANGELS' SONG

It came upon the midnight clear,
  That glorious song of old,
From angels bending near the earth
  To touch their harps of gold:
" Peace to the earth, goodwill to men
  From Heaven's all-gracious King:"
The world in solemn stillness lay
  To hear the angels sing.

Still through the cloven sky they come
  With peaceful wings unfurl'd;
And still their heavenly music floats
  O'er all the weary world:
Above its sad and lowly plains
  They bend on heavenly wing,
And ever o'er its Babel sounds
  The blessèd angels sing.

Yet with the woes of sin and strife
  The world has suffer'd long;
Beneath the angel strain have rolled
  Two thousand years of wrong;

And men, at war with men, hear not
    The love-song which they bring:
O! hush the noise, ye men of strife,
    And hear the angels sing!

And ye, beneath life's crushing load
    Whose forms are bending low,
Who toil along the climbing way
    With painful steps and slow;
Look now! for glad and golden hours
    Come swiftly on the wing:
O! rest beside the weary road,
    And hear the angels sing!

For lo! the days are hastening on,
    By prophet-bards foretold,
When with the ever-circling years
    Comes round the age of gold;
When Peace shall over all the earth
    Its ancient splendours fling,
And the whole world send back the song
    Which now the angels sing.
                        E. H. Sears

LXXI

THE STAR OF BETHLEHEM

When, marshall'd on the nightly plain,
    The glittering hosts bestud the sky;
One star alone of all the train
    Can fix the sinner's wandering eye.

Hark! hark! to God the chorus breaks
    From every host, from every gem;
But one alone the Saviour speaks,
    It is the star of Bethlehem.

Once on the raging seas I rode,
  The storm was loud, the night was dark,
The ocean yawn'd—and rudely blow'd
  The wind that toss'd my foundering bark :

Deep horror then my vitals froze,
  Death-struck, I ceased the tide to stem,
When suddenly a star arose,
  It was the star of Bethlehem.

It was my guide, my light, my all ;
  It bade my dark forebodings cease ;
And through the storm, and danger's thrall,
  It led me to the port of peace.

Now safely moor'd, my perils o'er,
  I'll sing first in night's diadem,
For ever and for evermore,
  The star ! the star of Bethlehem !
                              H. Kirke White

THE SEA OF GALILEE

LXXII

How pleasant to me thy deep blue wave,
  O sea of Galilee !
For the Glorious One, who came to save,
  Has often stood by thee.

Fair are the lakes in the land I love,
  Where pine and heather grow ;
But thou hast loveliness far above
  What Nature can bestow.

It is not that the wild gazelle
  Comes down to drink thy tide;
But He that was pierced to save from hell
  Oft wander'd by thy side.

It is not that the fig-tree grows,
  And palm, in thy soft air;
But that Sharon's fair and bleeding rose
  Once spread its fragrance there.

Graceful round thee the mountains meet,
  Thou calm, reposing sea;
But ah, far more! the beautiful feet
  Of Jesus walk'd o'er thee.

Those days are past—Bethsaida, where?
  Chorazin, where art thou?
His tent the wild Arab pitches there,
  The wild reeds shade thy brow.

Tell me, ye mould'ring fragments, tell,
  Was the Saviour's city here?
Lifted to heaven, has it sunk to hell,
  With none to shed a tear?

Ah! would my flock from thee might learn
  How days of grace will flee;
How all an offer'd Christ who spurn
  Shall mourn, at last, like thee.

And was it beside this very sea
  The new-risen Saviour said
Three times to Simon, "Lovest thou Me?
  My lambs and sheep then feed?"

O Saviour! gone to God's right hand!
   Yet the same Saviour still,
Graved on Thy heart is this lovely strand,
   And every fragrant hill.

O give me, Lord, by this sacred wave,
   Threefold Thy love divine,
That I may feed, till I find my grace,
   Thy flock—both Thine and mine.
R. M. McCheyne

LXXIII
SAINT ANDREW.

When brothers part for manhood's race,
   What gift may most enduring prove
To keep fond memory in her place,
   And certify a brother's love?

'Tis true, bright hours together told,
   And blissful dreams in secret shar'd,
Serene or solemn, gay or bold,
   Shall last in fancy unimpair'd.

E'en round the death-bed of the good
   Such dear remembrances will hover,
And haunt us with no vexing mood,
   When all the cares of earth are over.

But yet our craving spirits feel
   We shall live on, though fancy die,
And seek a surer pledge,—a seal
   Of love to last eternally.

Who art thou that wouldst grave thy name
   Thus deeply in a brother's heart?
Look on this saint, and learn to frame
   Thy love-charm with true Christian art.

First seek thy Saviour out, and dwell
   Beneath the shadow of His roof,
Till thou have scann'd His features well,
   And known Him for the Christ by proof;

Such proof as they are sure to find
   Who spend with Him their happy days,
Clean hands, and a self-ruling mind,
   Ever in time for love and praise.

Thus, potent with the spell of Heaven,
   Go, and thine erring brother gain;
Entice him home to be forgiven,
   Till he, too, see his Saviour plain.

Or, if before thee in the race,
   Urge him with thine advancing tread,
Till, like twin stars, with even pace,
   Each lucid course be duly sped.

No fading frail memorial give
   To soothe his soul when thou art gone,
But wreaths of hope for ay to live,
   And thoughts of good together done.

That so, before the judgment seat,
   Though chang'd and glorified each face,
Not unremember'd ye may meet
   For endless ages to embrace.

J. Keble

LXXIV
LAZARUS

When Lazarus left his charnel-cave,
  And home to Mary's house return'd,
  Was this demanded—if he yearn'd
To hear her weeping by his grave?

Where wert thou, Brother, those four days?
  There lives no record of reply,
  Which telling what it is to die
Had surely added praise to praise.

From every house the neighbours met,
  The streets were fill'd with joyful sound,
  A solemn gladness even crown'd
The purple brows of Olivet.

Behold a man raised up by Christ!
  The rest remaineth unreveal'd;
  He told it not; or something seal'd
The lips of that Evangelist.
A. Tennyson

LXXV
MARY

Her eyes are homes of silent prayer,
  Nor other thought her mind admits
  But he was dead, and there he sits,
And He that brought him back is there.

Then one deep love doth supersede
   All other, when her ardent gaze
   Roves from the living brother's face,
And rests upon the Life indeed.

All subtle thought, all curious fears,
   Borne down by gladness so complete,
   She bows, she bathes the Saviour's feet
With costly spikenard and with tears.

Thrice blest whose lives are faithful prayers,
   Whose loves in higher love endure;
   What souls possess themselves so pure,
Or is this blessedness like theirs?
A. Tennyson

LXXVI
THE WEDDING FEAST

Courage, O faithful heart;
   Steadfast for ever!
In the eternal love
   Faltering never:
Courage, O downcast eyes,
   Bitter tears shedding;
Hark! how the chimes ring out
   Joy for the wedding!

Open the golden doors;
   Through the high portal
Let the rich glory stream
   Sea-like, immortal!
Open the golden doors
   Wide from the centre;—
Countless the multitude
   Hither must enter!

Light up the palace halls,
  From roof-tree to basement,
Bid the warm festal glow,
  Flood every casement:
Chant ye the bridal song
  Solemn and holy,
Waking to Paradise
  Souls that lie lowly.

Out of old battle-fields
  No man remembers;
Out of still village yards
  And dank charnel-chambers,
From the chill ocean-graves
  Under far waters
And the dear sepulchres
  Where sleep the martyrs.

Dives and Lazarus
  One with the other;
Peasant and emperor,
  Foeman and brother,
Men with long century-lives
  Braving death's shadow,
And sweet baby blossoms—fresh
  As flower in the meadow:—

Out of the million haunts
  Where dead men lie idle,
Out of life's thousand ways:—
  Call to the bridal:
Open the golden doors
  Wide from the centre!
For they that are ready
  To glory shall enter!

W. E. Littlewood

LXXVII

THE GOOD SHEPHERD

Into a desolate land
  White with the drifted snow,
Into a weary land
  Our truant footsteps go :
Yet doth Thy care, O Father,
  Ever Thy wanderers keep ;
Still doth Thy love, O Shepherd,
  Follow Thy sheep

Over the pathless wild
  Do I not see Him come?
Him who shall bear me back,
  Him who shall lead me home ?
Listen ! between the storm-gusts
  Unto the straining ear,
Comes not the cheering whisper—
  "Jesus is near."

Over me He is bending !
  Now I can safely rest,
Found at the last, and clinging
  Close to the Shepherd's breast :
So let me lie till the fold-bells
  Sound on the homeward track,
And the rejoicing angels
  Welcome us back !

W. E. Littlewood

LXXVIII
THE TREASURE

Far away, where the tempests play,
  Over the lonely seas,
Sail or still, with a steady will,
  Onward before the breeze!

Onward yet, till our hearts forget
  The loves that we leave behind,
Till the memories dear, that thrill in our ear
  Flow past like the whistling wind!

Let them come, sweet thoughts of home,
  And voices we loved of old;—
What care we, that sail the sea,
  Bound for a Land of Gold?

Gems there are which are lovelier far
  Than the flash of a maiden's eyes;
Jewels bright, as the magic light
  That purples the evening skies.

Crowns that gleam like a fairy dream
  Treasures of price untold;
And we are bound for that charmèd ground,
  We sail for the Land of Gold!
                W. E. Littlewood

LXXIX
THE FOOLISH VIRGINS

Late, late, so late! and dark the night, and chill!
Late, late, so late! but we can enter still.
  Too late, too late, ye cannot enter now.

No light had we, for that we do repent ;
And learning this, the Bridegroom will relent.
   Too late, too late, ye cannot enter now.

No light, so late ! and dark and chill the night !
O let us in, that we may find the light !
   Too late, too late, ye cannot enter now.

Have we not heard the Bridegroom is so sweet ?
O, let us in, though late, to kiss His feet !
   No, no, too late ! ye cannot enter now.
A. Tennyson

LXXX
"UNTO HIM WHO HATH LOVED US"

There is no love like the love of Jesus,
   Never to fade or fall,
Till into the fold of the peace of God
   He has gather'd us all !

There is no heart like the heart of Jesus
   Fill'd with a tender lore ;
Not a throb nor throe our hearts can know
   But He suffer'd before !

There is no eye like the eye of Jesus
   Piercing far away :
Never out of the sight of its tender light
   Can the wanderer stray !

There is no voice like the voice of Jesus,
   Ah ! how sweet its chime,
Like the musical ring of some rushing spring
   In the summer-time !

O might we listen that voice of Jesus,
O might we never roam,
Till our souls should rest, in peace, on His breast,
In the Heavenly home !
W. E. Littlewood

LXXXI
"*I AM THE WAY, THE TRUTH, AND THE LIFE*"

Come, my way, my truth, my life :
Such a way, as gives us breath :
Such a truth, as ends all strife :
Such a life, as killeth death.

Come, my light, my feast, my strength :
Such a light, as shows a feast :
Such a feast, as mends in length :
Such a strength, as makes his guest.

Come, my joy, my love, my heart :
Such a joy as none can move :
Such a love, as none can part :
Such a heart, as joys in love.
G. Herbert

LXXXII
"*WE'VE NO ABIDING CITY HERE*"

We've no abiding city here :
This may distress the worldling's mind ;
But should not cost the saint a tear,
Who hopes a better rest to find.

We've no abiding city here:
  Sad truth, were this to be our home!
But let this thought our spirits cheer;
  We seek a city yet to come.

We've no abiding city here:
  Then let us live as pilgrims do!
Let not the world our rest appear,
  But let us haste from all below.

We've no abiding city here:
  We seek a city out of sight;
Zion its name, the Lord is there,
  It shines with everlasting light!

Zion! Jehovah is her strength;
  Secure she smiles at all her foes;
And weary travellers at length
  Within her sacred walls repose.

O! sweet abode of peace and love,
  Where pilgrims freed from toil are blest!
Had I the pinions of a dove,
  I'd flee away, and be at rest!
                                T. Kelly

LXXXIII

"A FOUNTAIN OPENED FOR SIN AND FOR UNCLEANNESS"

There is a fountain fill'd with blood
  Drawn from Emmanuel's veins;
And sinners, plunged beneath that flood,
  Lose all their guilty stains.

The dying thief rejoiced to see
　That fountain in His day ;
And there would I, as vile as he,
　Wash all my sins away.

Dear dying Lamb ! Thy precious Blood
　Shall never lose its power,
Till all the ransom'd church of God
　Be saved, to sin no more.

E'er since, by faith, I saw the stream
　Thy flowing wounds supply,
Redeeming love has been my theme,
　And shall be till I die.

Then in a nobler, sweeter song
　I'll sing Thy power to save,
When this poor lisping, stammering tongue
　Lies silent in the grave.

Lord, I believe Thou hast prepared,
　Unworthy though I be,
For me a blood-bought free reward,
　A golden harp for me :

'Tis strung and tuned for endless years,
　And form'd by power divine,
To sound in God the Father's ears,
　No other name but Thine.

　　　　　　　　　　W. Cowper

LXXXIV
CHRIST'S CHURCH UNIVERSAL
" My Name shall be great among the Gentiles"

Yes, so it was ere Jesus came;
Alternate then His altar flame
    Blazed up and died away;
And Silence took her turn with song,
And Solitude with the fair throng
    That own'd the festal day.
For in Earth's daily circuit then
    One only border
Reflected to the seraph's ken
    Heaven's light and order.

But now to the revolving sphere
We point, and say, no desert here,
    No waste so dark and lone,
But to the hour of sacrifice
Comes daily in its turn, and lies
    In light beneath the throne.
Each point of time, from morn to eve,
    From eve to morning,
The shrine doth from the spouse receive
    Praise and adorning.
J. Keble

LXXXV
THE MINISTRY OF ANGELS

And is there care in Heaven, and is there love
    In heavenly spirits to these creatures base,
That may compassion of their evils move?
    There is—else much more wretched were the case

Of men than beasts. But, O, the exceeding grace
Of highest God that loves His creatures so,
   And all His works with mercy doth embrace,
That blessed Angels He sends to and fro
To serve to wicked man, to serve His wicked foe.

How oft do they their silver bowers leave,
   To come to succour us who comfort want ;
How oft do they with golden pinions cleave
   The flitting skies like flying pursuivant,
   Against foul fiends to aid us militant.
They for us fight, they watch and duly ward,
   And their bright squadrons round about us plant,
And all for love, and nothing for reward :
   O, why should heavenly God to man have such
      regard?
                              E. Spenser

LXXXVI

LITTLE CHRISTEL

"*Be ye doers of the Word, and not hearers only*"

I.

Going home from the House of God,
   The flower at her foot, and the sun overhead,
Little Christel so thoughtfully trod,
   Pondering what the preacher had said.

" Even the youngest, humblest child,
   Something may do to please the Lord."
" Now what," thought she, and half sadly smiled,
   " Can I, so little and poor, afford?"

"Never, never, a day should pass
   Without some kindness, kindly shown."
Little Christel looked down at the grass
   Rising like incense before the throne.

"Well, a day is before me now,
   Yet what," thought she, "can I do if I try?
If an angel of God should show me how,
   But silly am I, and the hours they fly."

Then a lark sprang singing up from the sod,
   And Christel thought, as he rose to the blue,
"Perhaps he will carry my prayer to God,
   But who would have thought the little lark knew?"

II.

Now she entered the village street,
   With book in hand, and face demure,
And soon she came, with sober feet,
   To a crying babe at a cottage door.

The child had a windmill that would not move,
   It puff'd with its round red cheeks in vain,
One sail stuck fast in a puzzling groove,
   And baby's breath could not stir it again.

Poor baby beat the sail, and cried,
   While no one came from the cottage door;
But little Christel knelt down by its side,
   And set the windmill going once more.

Then babe was pleased, and the little girl
   Was glad when she heard it laugh and crow:
Thinking, happy windmill, that has but to whirl,
   To please the pretty young creature so.

III.

No thought of herself was in her head,
   As she pass'd out at the end of the street,
And came to a rose-tree, tall and red,
   Drooping and faint with the summer heat.

She ran to a brook that was flowing by ;
   She made of her two hands a nice round cup,
And wash'd the roots of the rose-tree high,
   Till it lifted its languid blossoms up.

"O happy brook!" thought little Christel,
   "You have done some good this summer's day,
You have made the flower look fresh and well;"
   Then she rose, and went on her way.

IV.

But she saw, as she walk'd by the side of the brook,
   Some great rough stones that troubled its course,
And the gurgling water seemed to say, "Look !
   I struggle, and tumble, and murmur hoarse !

"How these stones obstruct my road !
   How I wish they were off, and gone ;
Then I could flow, as once I flow'd,
   Singing in silvery undertone."

Then little Christel, as light as a bird,
   Put off the shoes from her young white feet ;
She moves two stones, she comes to the third,
   The brook already sings, "Thanks to you, sweet !"

O, then she hears the lark in the skies,
  And thinks, "What is it to God he says?"
And she stumbles, and falls, and cannot rise,
  For the water stifles her downward face.

The little brook flows on, as before,
  The little lark sings with as sweet a sound;
The little babe crows at the cottage door;
  And the red rose blooms, but Christel lies drown'd.

V.

Come in softly, this is the room;
  Is not that an innocent face?
Yes, those flowers give a faint perfume,—
  Think child, of Heaven, and the Lord His grace.

Three at the right, and three at the left,
  Two at the feet, and two at the head,
The tapers burn. The friends bereft,
  Have cried till their eyes are swollen and red.

Who would have thought it when little Christel
  Ponder'd on what the preacher had told?
But the good wise God does all things well,
  And the fair young creature lies dead and cold.

VI.

Then a little stream crept into the place,
  And rippled up to the coffin's side,
And touch'd the corpse on its pale round face,
  And kiss'd the eyes till they trembled wide;

Saying, "I am a river of joy from Heaven;
 You help'd the brook, and I help you,
I sprinkle your brow with life-drops seven,
 I bathe your eyes with healing dew."

Then a rose-branch in through the window came,
 And colour'd her cheeks and lips with red;
"I remember, and Heaven does the same,"
 Was all that the faithful rose-branch said.

Then a bright small form to her cold neck clung,
 It breath'd on her, till her breast did fill,
Saying, "I am a cherub, fond and young,
 And I saw who breathed on the baby's mill."

Then little Christel sat up and smil'd,
 And said, "Who put these flowers in my hand?"
And rubb'd her eyes, poor innocent child;
 Not being able to understand.

VII.

But soon she heard the big bell of the Church
 Give the hour, which made her say,
"Ah! I have slept and dream'd in the porch;
 It is a very drowsy day."

Anon

LXXXVII

KING ROBERT OF SICILY

"*He hath put down the mighty from their seat*"

Robert of Sicily, brother of Pope Urbane
And Valmond, emperor of Allemaine,
Apparell'd in magnificent attire,
With retinue of many a knight and squire,

On St. John's Eve, at vespers, proudly sat
And heard the priests chant the Magnificat,
And as he listened, o'er and o'er again
Repeated, like a burden, or refrain,
He caught the words " Deposuit potentes
De sede, et exaltavit humiles ;"
And slowly lifting up his kingly head,
He, to a learned clerk beside him, said,
"What mean these words?" The clerk made
      answer meet,
"He has put down the mighty from their seat,
And has exalted them of low degree."
Thereat king Robert mutter'd scornfully,
"'Tis well that such seditious words are sung
Only by priests, and in the Latin tongue:
For unto priests and people be it known,
There is no power can push me from my throne."
And leaning back he yawn'd and fell asleep,
Lull'd by the chant, monotonous and deep.

When he awoke it was already night,
The church was empty, and there was no light,
Save where the lamps, that glimmer'd few and faint,
Lighted a little space before some saint.
He started from his seat and gazed around,
He saw no living thing and heard no sound;
He grop'd toward the door, but it was lock'd—
He cried aloud, and listen'd, and then knock'd,
And utter'd awful threat'nings and complaints,
And imprecations upon men and saints.
The sounds re-echoed from the roof and walls,
As if dead priests were laughing in their stalls.

At length the sexton, hearing from without
The tumult of the knocking, and the shout,
And thinking thieves were in the house of prayer,
Came with his lantern, asking—"Who is there?"
Half choked with rage, king Robert fiercely said,
"Open: 'tis I, the king, art thou afraid?"
The frighten'd sexton flung the portal wide;
A man rush'd by him at a single stride—
Haggard, half naked, without hat or cloak—
Who neither turn'd, nor look'd at him, nor spoke,
But leap'd into the blackness of the night,
And, like a spectre, vanish'd from the sight.

Robert of Sicily, brother of Pope Urbane
And Valmond, emperor of Allemaine,
Despoil'd of his magnificent attire,
Bareheaded, breathless, and besprent with mire,
With sense of wrong and outrage desperate,
Strode on, and thunder'd at the palace gate,
Rush'd thro' the court-yard, thrusting in his rage
To right and left each seneschal and page,
Until at last he reach'd the banquet room,
Blazing with light, and breathing with perfume.

There on the dais sat another king,
Wearing his robes, his crown, his signet ring;
King Robert's self in features, form, and height,
But all transfigured with angelic light!
It was an angel; and his presence there
With a divine effulgence fill'd the air,
An exaltation piercing the disguise,
Though none the hidden angel recognise.
A moment speechless, motionless, amazed,

The throneless monarch on the angel gazed:
Who met his looks of anger and surprise
With the divine compassion of his eyes;
Then said, "Who art thou? and why com'st thou
    here?"
To which king Robert answer'd, with a sneer,
"I am the king, and come to claim my own
From an impostor, who usurps my throne."
The angel answer'd, with unruffled brow,
"Nay, not the king, but the king's jester; thou
Henceforth shalt wear the bells and scallop'd cape,
And for thy counsellor shalt lead an ape,
Thou shalt obey my servants when they call,
And wait upon my henchmen in the hall."
Deaf to king Robert's threats, and cries, and prayers,
They thrust him from the hall, and down the stairs;
It was no dream; the world he lov'd so much,
Had turn'd to dust and ashes at his touch.

Days came and went, and now return'd again
To Sicily, the old Saturnian reign;
Under the angel's governance benign
The happy island danced with corn and wine;
And deep within the mountain's burning breast
Enceladus the giant was at rest.
Meanwhile king Robert yielded to his fate,
Sullen, and silent, and disconsolate;
Dress'd in the motley garb that jesters wear,
Close shaven above the ears, with vacant stare,
His only friend the ape, his only food
What others left,—he still was unsubdued.
And when the angel met him on his way,
And half in earnest, half in jest would say,

Sternly, though tenderly, that he might feel
The velvet scabbard held a sword of steel,
"Art thou the king?" the passion of his woe
Burst from him, in resistless overflow,
And lifting high his forehead, he would fling
The passionate answer back, " I am, I am the king."
Almost three years were ended, when there came
Ambassadors of great repute and name
From Valmond, emperor of Allemaine,
Unto king Robert, saying that Pope Urbane
By letter summon'd them forthwith to come
On Holy Thursday to his city of Rome.
The angel with great joy received his guests,
And gave them presents of embroider'd vests. . . .
Then he departed with them o'er the sea,
Into the lovely land of Italy. . . .
And lo! among the menials, in mock state,
Upon a piebald steed with shambling gait,
His cloak of fox-tails flapping in the wind,
The solemn ape demurely perch'd behind,
King Robert rode, making huge merriment
In all the country towns thro' which they went.

The Pope received them with great pomp, and blare
Of banner'd trumpets, in St. Peter's Square;
Giving his benediction and embrace,
Fervent, and full of apostolic grace.
While, with congratulations and with prayers,
He entertain'd an angel unawares.

In solemn state the holy week went by,
And Easter Sunday gleam'd upon the sky;
The presence of the angel, with its light,
Before the sun rose, made the city bright,

And with new fervour fill'd the hearts of men,
Who felt that Christ was risen indeed again.
Even the jester on his bed of straw,
With haggard eyes the' unwonted splendour saw,
He felt within a power unfelt before,
And kneeling humbly on his chamber floor,
He heard the rushing garments of the Lord
Sweep through the silent air, ascending heavenward.

And now the visit ending, and once more
Valmond returning to the Danube shore,
Homeward the angel journey'd, and again
The land was made resplendent with his train,
Flashing along the towns of Italy
Unto Salerno, and from there by sea.
And when once more within Palermo's wall,
And seated on the throne in his great hall,
He heard the Angelus from convent towers,
As if the better world convers'd with ours,
He beckon'd to king Robert to draw nigher,
And with a gesture bade the rest retire ;
And when they were alone, the angel said,
"Art thou the king?" Then bowing down his head,
King Robert cross'd both hands upon his breast,
And meekly answer'd him, "Thou knowest best :
My sins as scarlet are ; let me go hence,
And in some cloister's school of penitence,
Across those stones that pave the way to heaven,
Walk barefoot, till my guilty soul is shriven!"
The angel smiled, and from his radiant face
A holy light illumin'd all the place,
And through the open window, loud and clear,
They heard the monks chant in the chapel near,

Above the stir and tumult of the street:
"He has put down the mighty from their seat,
And has exalted them of low degree!"
And through the chant, a second melody
Rose like the throbbing of a single string:
"I am an angel, and thou art the king!"
King Robert, who was standing near the throne,
Lifted his eyes, and lo! he was alone!
But all apparell'd as in days of old,
With ermin'd mantle, and with cloth of gold;
And when his courtiers came, they found him there,
Kneeling upon the floor, absorb'd in silent prayer.
H. W. Longfellow

LXXXVIII

CHARITY

Then constant faith, and holy hope shall die,
One lost in certainty, and one in joy;
Whilst thou, more happy power, fair Charity,
Triumphant sister, greatest of the three,
Thy office and thy nature still the same,
Lasting thy lamp, and unconsum'd thy flame,
Shalt still survive—
Shalt stand before the host of Heaven confess'd,
For ever blessing, and for ever blest.
Matthew Prior

LXXXIX
THE LAST TRUMP

As grew the power of sacred lays
　The spheres began to move,
And sung the great Creator's praise
　To all the bless'd above :
So when the last and dreadful hour
This crumbling pageant shall devour,
The trumpet shall be heard on high,
The dead shall live, the living die,
And music shall untune the sky.
　　　　　　　　　John Dryden

XC

"*And Jesus said unto them, There shall not be left here one stone upon another. . . Heaven and earth shall pass away.*"

The cloud-capp'd towers, the gorgeous palaces,
The solemn temples, the great globe itself,
Yea, all which it inherits shall dissolve :
And, like this insubstantial pageant faded,
Leave not a rack behind.　We are such stuff
As dreams are made of, and our little life
Is rounded with a sleep.
　　　　　　　　William Shakspeare

XCI
HOLY SCRIPTURE

Who has this Book and reads it not
  Doth God Himself despise ;
Who reads, but understandeth not,
  His soul in darkness lies.

Who understands, but savours not,
  He finds no rest in trouble ;
Who savours but obeyeth not,
  He hath his judgment double.

Who reads this book—who understands—
  Doth savour and obey—
His soul shall stand at God's right hand,
  In the great Judgment Day.
Old Hymn

IV

LIFE

XCII

THE PILGRIMAGE

Give me my scallop shell of quiet,
My staff of truth to walk upon,
My scrip of joy—immortal diet—
My bottle of salvation;
My gown of glory, hope's true gage;
And thus I'll take my pilgrimage,
While my soul, like a quiet palmer,
Travelleth toward the land of Heaven.
Sir Walter Raleigh

XCIII

THE HAPPY LIFE

How happy is he born and taught
   That serveth not another's will;
Whose armour is his honest thought,
   And simple truth his utmost skill;

Whose passions not his masters are,
   Whose soul is still prepared for death,
Untied unto the worldly care
   Of public fame, or private breath;

Who envies none that chance doth raise,
   Or vice; who never understood
How deepest wounds are given by praise,
   Nor rules of state, but rules of good;

Who hath his life from rumours freed,
   Whose conscience is his strong retreat;
Whose state can neither flatterers feed,
   Nor ruin make oppressors great;

Who God doth late and early pray,
   More of his grace than gifts to lend,
And entertains the harmless day,
   With a religious book or friend.

This man is freed from servile bands
   Of hope to rise, or fear to fall;
Lord of himself, though not of lands,
   And having nothing, yet hath all.
Sir Henry Wotton

XCIV
THE GOOD LIFE—LONG LIFE.

  It is not growing like a tree
  In bulk doth make men better be;
Or standing long an oak three hundred year,
To fall a log at last, dry, bald, and sere;
   A lily of a day
   Is fairer far in May,
  Although it fall and die that night,
  It was the plant and flower of light.
In small proportions we just beauties see,
And in short measures life may perfect be.
Ben Jonson

XCV
SIN

Lord, with what care hast thou begirt us round!
    Parents first season us: then schoolmasters
Deliver us to laws; they send us bound
    To rules of reason, holy messengers.

Pulpits and Sundays, sorrow dogging sin,
    Afflictions sorted, anguish of all sizes,
Fine nets and stratagems to catch us in
    Bibles laid open, millions of surprises.

Blessings beforehand, ties of gratefulness,
    The sound of glory ringing in our ears;
Without, our shame—within, our consciences;
    Angels and grace, eternal hopes and fears.

Yet all these fences, and their whole array,
One cunning bosom-sin blows quite away.
                          G. Herbert

XCVI
VIRTUE

Sweet day, so cool, so calm, so bright,
    The bridal of the earth and sky,
The dew shall weep thy fall to-night:
        For thou must die.

Sweet rose, whose hue, angry and brave,
    Makes the rash gazer wipe his eye,
Thy root is ever in its grave,
        And thou must die.

Sweet Spring, full of sweet days and roses
A box where sweets compacted lie,
My music shows ye have your closes
    And all must die.

Only a sweet and virtuous soul,
Like season'd timber never gives;
But though the whole world turn to coal,
    Then chiefly lives.
                  G. Herbert

XCVII

HOLY HABITS

Slowly fashioned, link by link,
    Slowly waxing strong,
Till the spirit never shrink,
    Save from touch of wrong.

Holy habits are thy wealth,
    Golden, pleasant chains;
Passing earth's prime blessing—health,
    Endless, priceless gains;

Holy habits give thee place
    With the noblest, best,
All most Godlike, of thy race,
    And with seraphs blest;

Holy habits are thy joy,
    Wisdom's pleasant ways,
Yielding good without alloy,
    Lengthening, too, thy days.

Seek them, Christian, night and morn,
Seek them noon and even ;
Seek them till thy soul be born
Without stains—in Heaven.

T. Davis

XCVIII
LITTLE THINGS

The flower is small that decks the field,
  The bee is small that bends the flower,
But flower and bee alike may yield
  Food for a thoughtful hour.

Essence and attributes of each
  For ends profound combine ;
And all they are, and all they teach,
  Springs from the mind Divine.

Is there who scorneth little things?
  As wisely might he scorn to eat
The food that bounteous Autumn brings
  In little grains of wheat.

Methinks, indeed, that such an one
  Few pleasures upon earth will find,
Where well nigh every good is won
  From little things combined.

The lark that in the morning air
  Amid the sunbeams mounts and sings ;
What lifted her so lightly there ?—
  Small feathers in her wings.

What form too, then the beauteous dyes
  With which all nature oft is bright,
Meadows and streams, woods, hills, and skies?—
  Minutest waves of light.

And when the earth is sere and sad
  From summer's over fervid reign;
How is she in fresh beauty clad?—
  By little drops of rain.

Yea, and the robe that Nature weaves,
  Whence does it every robe surpass?—
From little flowers, and little leaves,
  And little blades of grass.

O sure, who scorneth little things,
  If he were not a thoughtless elf,
Far above all that round him springs,
  Would scorn his little self.
                Thomas Davis

XCIX

THE LOST DAY

Lost! lost! lost!
  A gem of countless price,
Cut from the living rock,
  And graved in Paradise:
Set round with three times eight
  Large diamonds, clear and bright,
And each with sixty smaller ones,
  All changeful as the light.

Lost—where the thoughtless throng
  In Fashion's mazes wind,
Where trilleth folly's song,
  Leaving a sting behind.
Yet to my hand 'twas given,
  A golden harp to buy,
Such as the white-robed choir attune
  To deathless minstrelsy.

Lost! lost! lost!
  I feel all search is vain;
That gem of countless cost
  Can ne'er be mine again:
I offer no reward—
  For till these heartstrings sever,
I know that Heaven's entrusted gift
  Is reft away for ever.

But when the sea and land,
  Like burning scroll have fled,
I'll see it in His hand,
  Who judgeth quick and dead;
And when of scathe and loss
  That man can ne'er repair,
The dread inquiry meets my soul,
  What shall it answer there?

L. H. *Sigourney*

c

RELIGION NOT ADVERSE TO PLEASURE

Religion does not censure or exclude
Unnumbered pleasures harmlessly pursued;
To study, culture, and with artful toil,
To meliorate and tame the stubborn soil;

To give dissimilar, yet fruitful lands,
The grain, or herb, or plant, that each demands ;
To cherish virtue in an humble state,
And share the joys your bounty may create ;
To mark the matchless workings of the power
That shuts within its seed the future flower :
Bids these in elegance of form excel,
In colour these, and those delight the smell ;
Sends Nature forth, the daughter of the skies,
To dance on earth, and charm all human eyes :
To teach the canvass innocent deceit,
Or lay the landscape on the snowy sheet—
These, these are arts pursued without a crime,
That leave no stain upon the wing of time.
Cowper

CI

MUTABILITY

The sea of Fortune doth not even flow,
   She draws her favours to the lowest ebb,
Her tides have equal times to come and go,
   Her loom doth weave the fine and coarsest web.
No joy so great, but runneth to an end ;
No hap so hard, but may in time amend.

Not always full of leaf, nor always spring;
   Not endless night, yet not eternal day :
The saddest birds a season find to sing,
   The roughest storm a calm may soon allay.
Thus with succeeding turns, God tempereth all,
That man may hope to rise, yet fear to fall.
R. Southwell

CII
EARLY RISING AND PRAYER

When first thine eyes unveil, give thy soul leave
To do the like ; our bodies but forerun
    The spirit's duty : true hearts spread and heave
Unto their God as flowers do to the sun ;
      Give Him thy first thoughts then, so shalt thou keep
    Him company all day, and in Him sleep.

Yet never sleep the sun up ; prayer should
Dawn with the day : these are set awful hours
    'Twixt Heav'n and us ; the manna was not good
After sun-rising ; far day sullies flowers :
      Rise to prevent the sun ; sleep doth sins glut,
    And Heaven's gate opens when the world's is shut.

Walk with thy fellow creatures : note the hush
And whisperings amongst them. Not a spring
    Or leaf but hath his morning hymn ; each bush
And oak doth know I Am.—Canst thou not sing ?
      O leave thy cares and follies ! go this way
    And thou art sure to prosper all the day.
                              H. Vaughan

CIII
TO A CHILD

My fairest child, I have no song to give you ;
    No lark could pipe to skies so dull and grey :
Yet, 'ere we part, one lesson I can leave you
         For every day.

Be good, sweet maid, and let who will be clever ;
Do noble things, not dream them, all day long :
And so make life, death, and that vast for ever,
   One grand, sweet song.
      C. Kingsley

CIV
THE CHRISTIAN'S PROGRESS

Through sorrow's path, and danger's road,
 Amid the deepening gloom,
We, soldiers of an injured King,
 Are marching to the tomb.

There, when the turmoil is no more,
 And all our powers decay,
Our cold remains in solitude
 Shall sleep the years away.

Our labours done, securely laid
 In this our last retreat,
Unheeded, o'er our silent dust
 The storms of life shall beat.

Yet not thus lifeless, thus inane,
 The vital spark shall lie,
For o'er life's wreck that spark shall rise
 To see its kindred sky.

These ashes too, this little dust,
 Our Father's care shall keep,
Till the last angel rise, and break
 The long and dreary sleep.

There love's soft dew o'er every eye,
 Shall shed its mildest rays,
And the long silent dust shall burst
 With shouts of endless praise.
      H. Kirke White

CV
THE CHARITIES OF THE POOR

There is a thought so purely blest,
    That to its use I oft repair,
When evil breaks my spirit's rest,
    And pleasure is but varied care;
A thought to gild the stormiest skies,
    To deck with flowers the bleakest moor—
A thought whose home is paradise—
    The charities of poor to poor.

It were not for the rich to blame,
    If they, whom fortune seems to scorn,
Should vent their ill-content and shame
    On others less or more forlorn:
But, that the veriest needs of life
    Should be dispensed with freer hand,
Than all their stores and treasures rife—
    Is not for them to understand.

To give the stranger's children bread,
    Of your precarious board the spoil—
To watch your helpless neighbour's bed,
    And sleepless, meet the morrow's toil;
The gifts, not proffer'd once alone,
    The daily sacrifice of years—
And when all else to give is gone,
    The precious gifts of love and tears.

Therefore lament not honest soul!
    That Providence holds back from thee,
The means thou might'st so well control—
    The luxuries of charity.

Manhood is nobler, as thou art ;
  And should some chance thy coffers fill,
How art thou sure to keep thine heart,
  To hold unchang'd thy loving will?
Wealth, like all other power, is blind,
  And bears a poison in its core,
To taint the best, if feeble mind,
  And madden that debas'd before.
It is the battle, not the prize,
  That fills the hero's breast with joy ;
And industry the bliss supplies
  Which mere possession might destroy.
               R. M. Milnes

CVI
SAYING THE RESPONSES
" What is the Church, and what am I ? "
  A world to one poor sandy grain,
    A waste of sea and sky,
  To one frail drop of rain.
" What boots one feeble infant tone
  To the full choir denied, or given,
    Where millions round the throne
  Are chanting morn and even ? "
Nay, the kind watchers hearkening there
  Distinguish in the deep of song
    Each little wave, each air,
  Upon the faltering tongue.
Each half-note in the great Amen,
  Even by the utterer's self unheard,
    They store ; O fail not then
  To bring thy lowly word.
               J. Keble

CVII
SAYING THE CREED

Give me a tender spotless child,
   Rehearsing o'er at eve, or morn,
His chant of glory undefiled,
   The creed that with the Church was born.

Down be his earnest forehead cast,
   His slender fingers join'd for prayer,
With half a frown his eye seal'd fast,
   Against the world's intruding glare.

Who while his lips so gently move,
   And all his look is purpose strong,
Can say what wonders, wrought above,
   Upon his unstain'd fancy throng?

The world new framed, the Christ new born,
   The mother-maid, the cross, and grave,
The rising sun on Easter morn,
   The fiery tongues sent down to save.

The gathering Church, the font of life,
   The saints and mourners kneeling round;
The Day to end the body's strife,
   The Saviour in His people crown'd.

All in majestic march, and even,
   To the veil'd eye by turns appear,
True to their time as stars in Heaven,
   No morning dreams so still and clear.

And this is Faith, and thus she wins
   Her victory, day by day rehearsed,
Seal but thine eye to pleasant sins,
   Love's glorious world will on thee burst.

J. Keble

CVIII
LABOUR

Pause not to dream of the future before us :
Pause not to weep the wild cares that come o'er us
Hark how Creation's deep musical chorus,
    Unintermitting goes up into Heaven !
Never the ocean wave falters in flowing :
Never the little seed stops in its growing ;
More and more richly the rose-heart keeps glowing,
    Till from its nourishing stem it is riven.

" Labour is worship ! " the robin is singing :
" Labour is worship ! " the wild bee is ringing :
Listen ! that eloquent music upspringing
    Speaks to thy soul from out Nature's great heart.
From the dark cloud flows the life giving shower ;
From the rough sod blows the soft breathing flower ;
From the small insect the rich coral bower ;
    Only man, in the plan, shrinks from his part.

Labour is life !—'tis the still water faileth ;
Idleness ever despaireth, bewaileth ;
Keep the watch wound, for the dark rust assaileth !
    Flowers droop and die in the stillness of noon.
Labour is glory !—the flying cloud lightens ;
Only the waving wing changes and brightens ;
Idle hearts only the dark future frightens ;
    Play the sweet keys would'st thou keep them in tune !

Labour is rest—from the sorrows that greet us,
Rest from all petty vexations that meet us ;
Rest from sin promptings that ever entreat us ;

Rest from world syrens that lure us to ill.
Work—and pure slumbers shall wait on thy pillow
Work—thou shalt ride over care's coming billow,
Lie not down wearied 'neath woe's weeping willow,
  Work with a stout heart and resolute will.

Labour is health—lo ! the husbandman reaping,
How through his veins goes the life-current leap-
    ing !
How his strong arm in its stalwart pride sweeping,
  True as a sunbeam, the swift sickle guides,
Labour is wealth—in the sea the pearl groweth,
Rich the Queen's robe from the frail cocoon floweth,
From the fine acorn the strong forest bloweth,
  Temple, and statue, the marble block hides.

Droop not though shame, sin, and anguish are round
    thee ;
Bravely fling off the cold chain that hath bound
    thee ;
Look to yon blue heaven smiling beyond thee ;
  Rest not content in thy darkness—a clod.
Work—for some good, be it ever so slowly ;
Cherish some flower, be it ever so lowly ;
Labour—all labour is noble and holy,
  Let thy great deeds be thy prayer to thy God.
                    F. S. Osgood

CIX
CHEERFUL GIVING

Christ before thy door is waiting :
  Rouse thee, slave of earthly gold.
Lo, He comes, thy pomp abating,
  Hungry, thirsty, homeless cold :

Hungry, by whom saints are fed
With the eternal living Bread;
Thirsty, from whose pierced side,
Healing waters spring and glide;
Cold and bare He comes, who never
May put off His robe of light;
Homeless, who must dwell for ever
In the Father's bosom bright.

Think how new-born saints assembling
Daily 'neath the shower of fire,
To their Lord in hope and trembling,
Brought the choice of earth's desire.
Never incense cloud so sweet,
As before the Apostle's feet,
Rose, majestic seer, from thee,
Type of royal hearts and free,
Son of holiest consolation,
When thou turned'st thy land to gold,
And thy gold to strong salvation,
Leaving all, by Christ to hold.

Type of priest, and monarch, casting
All their crowns before the throne,
And the treasure everlasting
Heaping in the world unknown.
Now in gems their relics lie,
And their names in blazonry,
And their forms from storied panes
Gleam athwart their own lov'd fanes,
Each his several radiance flinging
On the sacred altar floor,
Whether great ones much are bringing,
Or their mite the mean and poor.

Bring thine all, thy choicest treasure,
  Heap it high, and hide it deep :
Thou shalt win o'erflowing measure,
  Thou shalt climb where skies are steep.
    For as Heaven's true only light
    Quickens all those forms so bright,
    So where bounty never faints,
    There the Lord is with His saints,
Mercy's sweet contagion spreading
  Far and wide from heart to heart;
From His wounds atonement shedding
  On the blessed widow's part.
J. Keble

CX

CHARITY

An ardent spirit dwells with Christian love,
The eagle's vigour in the pitying dove ;
'Tis not enough that we with sorrow sigh,
That we the wants of pleading man supply,
That we in sympathy with sufferers feel,
Nor hear a grief without a wish to heal :
Not these suffice—to sickness, pain, and woe,
The Christian spirit loves with aid to go ;
Will not be sought, waits not for want to plead,
But seeks the duty—nay, prevents the need ;
Her utmost aid to every ill applies,
And plants relief for coming miseries.
Crabbe

CXI
THE UNREGARDED TOILS OF THE POOR.

Alas! what secret tears are shed,
 What wounded spirits bleed:
What loving hearts are sunderèd,
 And yet man takes no heed!

He goeth in his daily course,
 Made fat with oil and wine,
And pitieth not the weary souls
 That in his bondage pine—
That turn for him the mazy wheel,
 That delve for him the mine!
And pitieth not the children small
 In smoky factories dim,
That all day long, lean, pale, and faint,
 Do heavy tasks for him!

To him they are but as the stones
 Beneath his feet that lie:
It entereth not his thoughts that they
 With him claim sympathy:
It entereth not his thoughts that God
 Heareth the sufferer's groan,
That in His righteous eye their life
 Is precious as his own.
M. Howitt

CXII

SUNDAY

O day most calm, most bright!
The fruit of this, the next world's bud,
Th' indorsement of supreme delight,
Writ by a Friend, and with His blood:
The couch of time; care's balm and bay;
The week were dark but for thy light,
   Thy touch doth show the way.

Sundays the pillars are,
On which Heaven's palace archèd lies:
The other days fill up the spare
And hollow room with vanities,
They are the fruitful bed and borders
In God's rich garden: that is bare
   Which parts their ranks and orders.

The Sundays of man's life,
Threaded together on time's string,
Make bracelets to adorn the wife
Of the eternal, glorious King.
On Sunday Heaven's gate stands ope;
Blessings are plentiful and rife,
   More plentiful than hope.
G. Herbert

CXIII

THE HOUR OF PRAYER

Child, amid'st the flowers at play,
While the red light fades away:
Mother, with thine earnest eye
Ever following silently:
Father, by the breeze of eve
Call'd thy harvest-work to leave—
Pray! ere yet the dark hours be,
Lift the heart, and bend the knee.

Traveller in the stranger's land,
Far from thine own household band:
Mourner, haunted by the tone
Of a voice from this world gone:
Captive, in whose narrow cell
Sunshine hath not leave to dwell:
Sailor, on the darkening sea,
Lift the heart, and bend the knee.

Warrior, that from battle won
Breathest now at set of sun;
Woman, o'er the lowly slain,
Weeping on his burial plain:
Ye that triumph, ye that sigh
Kindred by one holy tie,
Heaven's first star alike ye see,
Lift the heart, and bend the knee.
                        F. Hemans

CXIV

`EVENING`

Behold the sun, that seem'd but now
    Enthronèd over head,
Beginning to decline below
    The globe whereon we tread;
And he, whom yet we look upon
    With comfort and delight,
Will quite depart from hence anon,
    And leave us to the night.

Thus time, unheeded, steals away
    The life which nature gave,
Thus are our bodies every day
    Declining to the grave:
Thus from us all our pleasures fly
    Whereon we set our heart,
And then the night of death draws nigh;
    Thus will they all depart.

Lord! though the sun forsake our sight,
    And mortal hopes are vain,
Let still Thine everlasting light
    Within our souls remain!
And in the nights of our distress
    Vouchsafe those rays divine
Which from the Sun of righteousness
    For ever brightly shine.

G. Withers

CXV

BAPTISMAL HYMN

In token that thou shalt not fear
    Christ crucified to own,
We print the cross upon thee here,
    And stamp thee His alone.

In token that thou shalt not blush
    To glory in His name,
We blazon here upon thy front
    His glory and His shame.

In token that thou shalt not flinch
    Christ's quarrel to maintain,
But 'neath His banner manfully
    Firm at thy post remain ;

In token that thou too shalt tread
    The path He travell'd by,
Endure the cross, despise the shame,
    And sit thee down on high ;

Thus outwardly, and visibly,
    We seal thee for His own :
And may the brow that wears His cross
    Hereafter share His crown.

H. Alford

CXVI
WATCHMAN, WHAT OF THE NIGHT?

Say, watchman, what of the night?
　Do the dews of the morning fall?
Have the orient skies a border of light,
　Like the fringe of a funeral pall?

" The night is fast waning on high,
　And soon shall the darkness flee,
And the morn shall spread o'er the blushing sky,
　And bright shall its glories be."

But, watchman, what of the night,
　When sorrow and pain are mine,
And the pleasures of life, so sweet and bright,
　No longer around me shine?

" That night of sorrow thy soul
　May surely prepare to meet;
But away shall the clouds of thy heaviness roll,
　And the morning of joy be sweet."

But, watchman, what of the night
　When the arrow of death is sped,
And the grave, which no glimmering star can light,
　Shall be my sleeping bed?

" That night is near, and the cheerless tomb
　Shall keep thy body in store,
Till the morn of eternity rise on the gloom,
　And night shall be no more."
　　　　　　　　　　Anon.

CXVII

THE MARINER'S HYMN

Launch thy bark, mariner! Christian, Heaven speed thee,
Let loose the rudder bands! good angels lead thee!
Set thy sails warily, tempests will come:
Steer thy course steadily! Christian, steer home!

Look to the weather bow, breakers are round thee!
Let fall the plummet now, shallows may ground thee!
Reef in the fore-sail there! hold the helm fast!
So—let the vessel wear! there swept the blast.

What of the night, watchman? what of the night?
"Cloudy—all quiet—no land yet—all's right."
Be wakeful, be vigilant, danger may be
At an hour when all seems securest to thee.

How—gains the leak so fast? clear out the hold,
Hoist up thy merchandise—heave out the gold!
There—let the ingots go! now the ship rights;
Hurrah! the harbour's near,—lo the red lights.

Slacken not sail yet at inlet or island,
Straight for the beacon steer—straight for the highland;
Crowd all thy canvass on, cut through the foam,
Christian! cast anchor now: Heaven is thy home!

C. Southey

CXVIII

MY PSALM

I mourn no more my vanish'd years:
  Beneath a tender rain,
An April rain of smiles and tears,
  My heart is young again.

The west winds blow, and singing low,
  I hear the glad streams run,
The windows of my soul I throw
  Wide open to the sun.

No longer forward, nor behind,
  I look in hope and fear:
But grateful, take the good I find,
  The best of now, and here.

I plough no more a desert land
  For harvest, weed and tare;
The manna dropping from God's hand
  Rebukes my painful care.

I break my pilgrim staff, I lay
  Aside the toiling oar;
The angel sought so far away
  I welcome at my door.

The airs of spring may never play
  Among the ripening corn,
Nor freshness of the flowers of May
  Blow through the autumn morn;

Yet shall the blue-eyed gentian look
  Through fringèd lids to heaven,
And the pale aster in the brook
  Shall see its image given;

The woods shall wear their robes of praise,
  The south wind softly sigh,
And sweet calm days in golden haze
  Melt down the amber sky.

Not less shall manly deed and word
  Rebuke an age of wrong:
The graven flowers that wreathe the sword
  Make not the blade less strong.

Enough that blessings undeserv'd
  Have mark'd my erring track,
That wheresoe'er my feet have swerv'd,
  His chastening turn'd me back.

That more and more a Providence
  Of love is understood,
Making the springs of time and sense
  Sweet with eternal good.

That death seems but a cover'd way,
  Which opens into light,
Wherein no blinded child can stray
  Beyond the Father's sight.

That care and trial seem at last,
  Through memory's sunset air,
Like mountain ranges overpast
  In purple distance fair.

That all the jarring notes of life
  Seem blending in a psalm,
And all the angles of its strife
  Slow rounding into calm.

And so the shadows fall apart,
  And so the west winds play;
And all the windows of my heart
  I open to this day.
J. G. Whittier

CXIX

YOUTH AND AGE

The seas are quiet when the winds are o'er,
So calm are we when passions are no more!
For then we know how vain it was to boast
Of fleeting things, so certain to be lost.

Clouds of affection from our younger eyes
Conceal that emptiness which age descries;
The soul's dark cottage, batter'd and decay'd,
Lets in new light through chinks that time has made.

Stronger by weakness, wiser men become
As they draw near to their eternal home;
Leaving the old, both worlds at once they view,
That stand upon the threshold of the new.
Waller

CXX
MY BIRD

Ere last year's moon had left the sky,
  A birdling sought my Indian nest,
And folded, O! so lovingly,
  Its tiny wings upon my breast.

From morn till evening's purple tinge,
  In winsome helplessness she lies;
Two rose leaves, with a silken fringe,
  Shut softly on her starry eyes.

There's not in Ind a lovelier bird;
  Broad earth owns not a happier nest:
O God, Thou hast a fountain stirred,
  Whose waters nevermore shall rest!

This beautiful, mysterious thing,
  This seeming visitant from Heaven,
This bird with the immortal wing,
  To me—to me, Thy hand has given.

The pulse first caught its tiny stroke,
  The blood its crimson hue, from mine:
This life, which I have dared invoke,
  Is parallel henceforth with mine.

A silent awe is in my room—
  I tremble with delicious fear;
The future, with its light, and gloom,
  Time, and eternity are here.

Doubts, hopes, in eager tumult rise:
  Hear, O my God! one earnest prayer;
Room for my bird in Paradise,
  And give her angel plumage there!

E. Judson

CXXI

HEAVEN

This world is all a fleeting show,
    For man's illusion given :
The smiles of joy, the tears of woe
Deceitful shine, deceitful flow ;
    There's nothing true but Heaven !

And false the light on glory's plume,
    As fading hues of even ;
And love, and hope, and beauty's bloom,
Are blossoms gathered from the tomb ;
    There's nothing bright but Heaven !

Poor wanderers of a stormy day,
    From wave to wave we're driven ;
And fancy's flash, and reason's ray,
Serve but to light the troubled way ;
    There's nothing calm but Heaven !
                      T. Moore

CXXII

DIFFERENT MINDS

Some murmur when their sky is clear
    And wholly bright to view,
If one small speck of dark appear
    In their great heaven of blue :
And some with thankful love are fill'd
    If but one streak of light,
One ray of God's good mercy, gild
    The darkness of their night.

In palaces are hearts that ask,
  In discontent and pride,
Why life is such a dreary task,
  And all good things denied:
And hearts in poorest huts admire
  How Love has in their aid
(Love that not ever seems to tire)
  Such rich provision made.
                Archbishop Trench

CXXIII

THE RULE OF GOD

I say to thee—Do thou repeat
To the first man thou mayest meet
In lane, highway, or open street,

That he and we and all men move
Under a canopy of love,
As broad as the blue sky above;

That doubt and trouble, fear and pain,
And anguish, all are shadows vain,
That death itself shall not remain;

That weary deserts we may tread,
A dreary labyrinth may thread,
Through dark ways underground be led;

Yet, if we will one Guide obey,
The dreariest path, the darkest way,
Shall issue out in heavenly day;

And we, on divers shores now cast,
Shall meet, our perilous voyage past,
All in our Father's house at last.

And ere thou leave him, say thou this:
Yet one word more—They only miss
The winning of that perfect bliss,

Who will not count it true, that love—
Blessing, not cursing,—rules above.
And that in it we live and move.

And one thing further make him know:
That to believe these things are so,
This firm faith never to forego—

Despite of all that seems at strife
With blessing, all with curses rife,—
That this is blessing, this is life.
Archbishop Trench

CXXIV

WRITTEN IN FRIAR'S CAVE HERMITAGE, ON NITHSIDE

Thou whom chance may hither lead,—
Be thou clad in russet weed,
Be thou deck'd in silken stole,
Grave these counsels on thy soul.

Life is but a day at most,
Sprung from night, in darkness lost,
Hope not sunshine every hour,
Fear not clouds will always lower.

As thy day grows warm and high,
Life's meridian flaming high,
Dost thou spurn the humble vale?
Life's proud summits would'st thou scale?
Check thy climbing step elate,
Evils lurk in felon wait :
Dangers eagle-pinion'd, bold,
Soar around each cliffy hold,
While cheerful peace with linnet song,
Chants the lowly dells among.

As the shades of evening close,
Beckoning thee to long repose ;
As life itself becomes disease,
Seek the chimney nook of ease,
And teach the sportive young ones round
Saws of experience wise and sound,
Say man's true genuine estimate,
The grand criterion of his fate,
Is not, Art thou high, or low?
Did thy fortune ebb or flow?
Did many talents gild thy span,
Or frugal nature grudge thee one?
Tell them, and press it on their mind,
As thou thyself must shortly find,
The smile or frown of awful Heaven
To virtue or to vice is given.
Say, to be just, and kind, and wise,
There solid self-enjoyment lies ;
That foolish, selfish, faithless ways,
Lead to the wretched, vile, and base.

Thus, resign'd and quiet, creep
To the bed of lasting sleep ;

Sleep, whence thou shalt ne'er awake,
Night, whose dawn shall never break,
Till future life, future no more,
To light, and joy the good restore,
To light and joy unknown before!

Stranger, go, Heaven be thy guide,
Quod the beadsman of Nithside.
Robert Burns

CXXV

THE COUNTRY CLERGYMAN

Near yonder copse, where once the garden smiled,
And still where many a garden flower grows wild;
There, where a few torn shrubs the place disclose,
The village preacher's modest mansion rose.
A man he was to all the country dear,
And passing rich with forty pounds a year.
Remote from towns, he ran his godly race,
Nor e'er had chang'd, nor wish'd to change his place;
Unskilful he to fawn, or look for power,
By doctrines fashion'd to the varying hour;
Far other aims his heart had learn'd to prize,
More bent to raise the wretched than to rise.
His house was known to all the vagrant train—
He chid their wanderings, but reliev'd their pain:
The long remember'd beggar was his guest,
Whose beard, descending, swept his aged breast;

The ruined spendthrift, now no longer proud,
Claim'd kindred there, and had his wants allow'd :
The broken soldier, kindly bade to stay,
Sat by his fire, and talk'd the night away ;
Wept o'er his wounds, or, tales of sorrow done,
Shoulder'd his crutch, and show'd how fields were
        won.
Pleas'd with his guests, the good man learnt to glow,
And quite forgot their vices in their woe ;
Careless their merits or their wants to scan,
His pity gave, ere charity began.
   Thus to relieve the wretched was his pride,
And e'en his failings lean'd to virtue's side ;
But in his duty prompt, at every call,
He watch'd and wept, he pray'd and felt for all.
And as a bird each fond endearment tries
To tempt its new-fledg'd offspring to the skies,
He tried each art, reprov'd each dull delay,
Allur'd to brighter worlds, and led the way.
Beside the bed where parting life was laid,
And sorrow, guilt, and pain, by turns dismay'd,
The reverend champion stood. At his control,
Despair and anguish fled the struggling soul ;
Comfort came down the trembling wretch to raise,
And his last faltering accents whisper'd praise.
   At church, with meek and unaffected grace,
His looks adorn'd the venerable place ;
Truth from his lips prevail'd with double sway,
And fools who came to scoff remain'd to pray.
The service past, around the pious man
With ready zeal each honest rustic ran ;
E'en children follow'd with endearing wile,
And pluck'd his gown to share the good man's smile.

L

His ready smile a parent's warmth express'd ;
Their welfare pleas'd him, and their cares distress'd :
To them his heart, his love, his griefs were given,
But all his serious thoughts had rest in heaven.
As some tall cliff that lifts its awful form,
Swells from the vale, and midway leaves the storm,
Though round its breast the rolling clouds are spread,
Eternal sunshines settles on its head.

O. Goldsmith

CXXVI

WILLIAM OF WYKEHAM AND HIS WORKS

In the days of our forefathers, the gallant days of old,
When Cressy's wondrous tale in Europe's ears was told ;
When the brave and gentle Prince, with his heroic peers,
Met France and all her knighthood in the vineyards of Poictiers ;
When captive kings on Edward's state right humbly did attend ;
When England's chivalry began the gartered knee to bend ;
Then in the foremost place, among the noblest of the land,
Stood Wykeham, the great Bishop, upon the king's right hand.

But when gracious Edward slept, and Richard wore
    the crown,
Forth came good William Wykeham, and meekly
    knelt him down.
Then out spake young King Richard: "What boon
    can Wykeham ask,
Which can surpass his worth, or our bounty over-
    task?
For art thou not our Chancellor? and where in all
    the realm
Is a wiser man or better, to guide the labouring
    helm?
And thou know'st the holy lore, and the mason's
    cunning skill:
So speak the word, good Wykeham, for thou shalt
    have thy will."

"I ask not wealth nor honour," the Bishop lowly
    said,
"Too much of both thy grandsire's hand heaped on
    a poor monk's head:
This world it is a weary load, it presses down my
    soul;
Fain would I pay my vows, and to Heav'n restore
    the whole.
Grant me that two fair Colleges, beneath thy
    charters sure,
At Oxford and at Winchester, for ever may
    endure,
Which Wykeham's hands shall raise upon the
    grassy sod,
In the name of Blessed Mary, and for the love of
    God."

The king he sealed the charters, and Wykeham traced the plan,
And God, Who gave him wisdom, prospered the lowly man:
So two fair Colleges arose, one in calm Oxford's glade,
And one where Itchen sparkles beneath the plane-tree shade.
There seventy true-born English boys he nourished year by year
In the nurture of good learning, and in God's holy fear;
And gave them steadfast laws, and bade them never move
Without sweet sign of brotherhood and gentle links of love.

They grew beside his pastoral throne, and kept his counsels sage,
And the good man rejoiced to bear such fruit in his old age:
He heard the pealing notes of praise, which morn and evening rung
Forth from their vaulted chapel, by their clear voices sung;
His eye beheld them two by two their comely order keep
Along the Minster's sacred aisles, and up the beech-crowned steep;
And, when he went to his reward, they shed the pious tear,
And sang the hallowed requiem over his saintly bier.

Then came the dark and evil time, when English
    blood was shed
All over fertile England, for the White Rose or the
    Red ;
But still in Wykeham's chapel the notes of praise
    were heard,
And still in Wykeham's College they taught the
    Sacred Word ;
And in the grey of morning, on every saint's-day
    still,
That black-gowned troop of brothers was winding
    up the hill :
There in the hollow trench, which the Danish pirate
    made,
Or through the broad encampment, the peaceful
    scholars played.

Trained in such gentle discipline from childhood to
    their prime
Grew mighty men and merciful, in that distracted
    time ;
Men on whom Wykeham's mantle fell, who stood
    beside their king
Even in his place, and bore his staff and the same
    pastoral ring ;
Who taught Heav'n-destined monarchs to emulate
    his deeds
Upon the banks of Cam, and in Eton's flowery
    meads ;
Founders of other Colleges by Cherwell's lilied
    side,
Who laid their bones with his, when in ripe old age
    they died.

And after that, when love grew cold, and Christendom was rent,
And sinful Churches laid them down in sackcloth to repent ;
When impious men bore sway, and wasted church and shrine
And cloister and old abbey, the works of men divine ;
Though upon all things sacred their robber hands they laid,
They did not tear from Wykeham's gates the Blessed Mother-Maid :
But still in Wykeham's cloisters fair wisdom did increase,
And then his sons began to learn the golden songs of Greece.

And all through great Eliza's reign, those days of pomp and pride,
They kept the laws of Wykeham, and did not swerve aside :
Still in their vaulted chapel, and in the Minster fair,
And in their lamplit chambers, they said the frequent prayer :
And when the Scottish plague-spot ran withering through the land,
The sons of Wykeham knelt beneath meek Andrewes' fostering hand,
And none of all the faithless, who swore th' unhallowed vow,
Drank of the crystal waters beneath the plane-tree bough.

Dread was the hour, but short as dread, when from
   the guarded down
Fierce Cromwell's rebel soldiery kept watch o'er
   Wykeham's town :
Beneath their pointed cannon all Itchen's valley
   lay,
St. Catharine's breezy side, and the woodlands far
   away,
The huge Cathedral sleeping in venerable gloom,
The modest College-tower, and the bedesmen's
   Norman home.
They spoiled the graves of valiant men, warrior
   and saint and sage,
But at the grave of Wykeham good angels quenched
   their rage.

Good angels still were there, when the base-hearted
   son
Of Charles, the royal martyr, his course of shame
   did run :
Then in those cloisters holy Ken strengthened with
   deeper prayer
His own and his dear scholars' souls to what pure
   souls should dare ;
Bold to rebuke enthronèd sin, with calm undazzled
   faith,
Whether amid the pomp of courts, or on the bed of
   death ;
Firm against kingly terrors in his free country's
   cause,
Faithful to God's anointed against a world's ap-
   plause.

Since then, what wars, what tumults, what change has Europe seen!
But never since in Itchen's vale has war or tumult been.
God's mercies have been with us, His favour still has blest
The memories sweet and glorious deeds of the good men at rest:
The many prayers, the daily praise, the nurture in the Word,
Have not in vain ascended up before the gracious Lord:
Nations, and thrones, and reverend laws, have melted like a dream;
Yet Wykeham's works are green and fresh beside the crystal stream.

Four hundred years and fifty their rolling course have sped
Since the first serge-clad scholar to Wykeham's feet was led;
And still his seventy faithful boys, in these presumptuous days,
Learn the old truths, speak the old words, tread in the ancient ways:
Still for their daily orisons resounds the matin chime;
Still linked in bands of brotherhood St. Catharine's steep they climb;
Still to their Sabbath worship they troop by Wykeham's tomb;
Still in the summer twilight sing their sweet song of Home.

And at th' appointed seasons, when Wykeham's
  bounties claim
The full heart's solemn tribute from those who love
  his name,
Still shall his white-robed children, as age on age
  rolls by,
At Oxford and at Winchester, give thanks to God
  most High:
And amid kings and martyrs shedding down
  glorious light,
While the deep-echoing organ swells to the vaulted
  height,
With grateful thoughts o'erflowing at the mercies
  they behold,
They shall praise their sainted fathers, the famous
  men of old.

CXXVII

TRUST IN GOD, AND DO THE RIGHT

Courage, brother, do not stumble,
  Though thy path be dark as night;
There's a star to guide the humble;—
  " Trust in God, and do the right."

Let the road be rough and dreary,
  And its end far out of sight,
Foot it bravely! strong, or weary,
  " Trust in God, and do the right."

Perish policy and cunning!
  Perish all that fears the light!
Whether losing, whether winning,
  "Trust in God, and do the right."

Trust no party, sect, or faction;
  Trust no leaders in the fight;
But in every word and action,
  "Trust in God, and do the right."

Trust no lovely forms of passion:
  Fiends may look like angels bright;
Trust no custom, school, or fashion,
  "Trust in God, and do the right."

Simple rule, and safest guiding,
  Inward peace, and inward might,
Star upon our path abiding,
  "Trust in God, and do the right."

Some will hate thee, some will love thee,
  Some will flatter, some will slight:
Cease from man, and look above thee,
  "Trust in God, and do the right."

Norman Macleod

V

DEATH

CXXVIII
MAN'S MORTALITY

Like as the damask rose you see,
Or as the blossom on the tree,
Or like the dainty flower of May,
Or like the morning to the day,
Or like the sun, or like the shade,
Or like the gourd which Jonas had,
E'en such is man;—whose thread is spun,
Drawn out, and cut, and so is done.—
The rose withers, the blossom blasteth,
The flower fades, the morning hasteth,
The sun sets, the shadow flies,
The gourd consumes—and man, he dies.
Like to the grass that's newly sprung,
Or like a tale that's new begun,
Or like the bird that's here to-day,
Or like the pearlèd dew of May,
Or like an hour, or like a span,
Or like the singing of a swan,
E'en such is man;—who lives by breath,
Is here, now there, in life, and death.—

The Sunday

The grass withers, the tale is ended,
The bird is flown, the dews ascended,
The hour is short, the span not long,
The swan's near death,—man's life is done.
S. Wastell

CXXIX
TO GOD IN HIS SICKNESS

What though my harp and viol be
Both hung upon the willow tree?
What though my bed be now my grave,
And for my house I darkness have?
What though my healthful days are fled,
And I lie number'd with the dead?
Yet I have hope, by Thy great power,
To spring—though now a wither'd flower.
R. Herrick

CXXX
A HAPPY DEATH

As precious gums are not for lasting fire,
They but perfume the temple, and expire;
So was she born, exhaled, and vanish'd hence,
A short sweet odour, of a vast expense.
She vanished, we can scarcely say she died;
For but a *now* did heaven and earth divide;
She pass'd serenely with a single breath;
This moment perfect health, the next was death.
As gentle dreams on waking thoughts pursue;
Or one dream pass'd, we slide into a new;

So close they follow, such wild order keep,
We think ourselves awake, and are asleep,
So softly death succeeded life in her,
She did but dream of Heaven, and she was there.
No pains she suffer'd, nor expired with noise ;
Her soul was whisper'd out with God's still voice.
John Dryden

CXXXI

MAGDALEN'S HYMN

During the Plague

The air of death breathes through our souls,
    The dead all round us lie ;
By day and night the death-bell tolls,
    And says, " Prepare to die."

The face that, in the morning sun,
    We thought so wondrous fair,
Hath faded, ere his course was run,
    Beneath its golden hair.

I see the old man in his grave
    With thin locks silvery-grey ;
I see the child's bright tresses wave
    In the cold breath of day.

The loving ones we loved the best,
    Like music, all are gone !
And the wan moonlight bathes in rest
    Their monumental stone.

But not, when the death prayer is said,
    The life of life departs ;
The body in the grave is laid,
    Its beauty in our hearts.

At holy midnight, voices sweet
    Like fragrance fill the room,
And happy ghosts with noiseless feet
    Come bright'ning from the tomb.

We know who sends the visions bright,
    From whose dear side they came !—
We veil our eyes before Thy light,
    We bless our Saviour's name.

This frame of dust, this feeble breath,
    The plague may soon destroy ;
We think on Thee, and feel in death
    A deep and awful joy.

Dim is the light of vanish'd years
    In the glory yet to come ;
O idle grief ! O foolish tears !
    When Jesus calls us home.

Like children for some bauble fair
    That weep themselves to rest ;
We part with life—awake ! and there
    The jewel in our breast.

Prof. Wilson

CXXXII

HOPE IN DEATH

My life's a shade, my days
Apace to death decline ;
My Lord is Life, He'll raise
My dust again, e'en mine.
　Sweet truth to me!
　　I shall arise,
　　And with these eyes
　My Saviour see.

My peaceful grave shall keep
My bones till that sweet day ;
I wake from my long sleep
And leave my bed of clay.
　Sweet truth to me!
　　I shall arise,
　　And with these eyes
　My Saviour see.

My Lord His angels shall
Their golden trumpets sound,
At whose most welcome call
My grave shall be unbound.
　Sweet truth to me!
　　I shall arise,
　　And with these eyes
　My Saviour see.

I said sometimes with tears,
Ah me! I'm loth to die!
Lord, silence Thou these fears:
My life's with Thee on high.
   Sweet truth to me!
     I shall arise,
      And with these eyes
   My Saviour see.

What means my trembling heart,
To be thus shy of death?
My life and I shan't part,
Though I resign my breath.
   Sweet truth to me!
     I shall arise,
      And with these eyes
   My Saviour see.

Then welcome, harmless grave:
By thee to Heaven I'll go:
My Lord His death shall save
Me from the flames below.
   Sweet truth to me!
     I shall arise,
      And with these eyes
   My Saviour see.

S. Crossman

CXXXIII
TO A DYING CHRISTIAN

Happy soul! thy days are ended,
 All thy mourning days below ;
Go, by angel guards attended,
 To the sight of Jesus go !
Waiting to receive thy spirit,
 Lo, the Saviour stands above,
Shews the purchase of His merit,
 Reaches out the crown of love !

Struggle through thy latest passion
 To thy dear Redeemer's breast,
To His uttermost salvation,
 To His everlasting rest !
For the joy He sets before thee,
 Bear a momentary pain ;
Die, to live the life of glory ;
 Suffer, with thy Lord to reign !
                    Charles Wesley

CXXXIV
A REAL OCCURRENCE IN A CIRCLE OF FRIENDS

Which is the happiest death to die?
" O !" said one, "if I might choose
Long at the gate of bliss would I lie,
And feast my spirit, ere it fly,
 With bright celestial views.

Mine were a lingering death without pain,
   A death which all might love to see,
   And mark how bright and sweet should be
The victory I should gain!

" Fain would I catch a hymn of love
   From the angel-harps which ring above:
   And sing it as my parting breath
   Quiver'd and expired in death—
   So that those on earth might hear
   The harp-notes of another sphere,
   And mark, when nature faints and dies,
   What springs of heavenly life arise,
   And gather from the death they view
   A ray of hope to light them through,
   When they shall be departing too."

   "No," said another, "so not I,
Sudden as thought is the death I would die;
I would suddenly lay my shackles by,
   Nor bear a single pang at parting,
   Nor see the tear of sorrow starting,
   Nor hear the quivering lips that bless me,
   Nor feel the hands of love that press me,
Nor the frame with mortal terror quaking,
Nor the heart where love's soft bands are breaking—
     So would I die!
   All bliss, without a pang to cloud it!
   All joy, without a pain to shroud it!
   Not slain, but caught up, as it were,
   To meet the Saviour in the air!
     So would I die!

O, how bright
Were the realms of light,
Bursting at once upon my sight !
Even so
I long to go,
These passing hours how sad and slow ! "

His voice grew faint, and fix'd was his eye,
As if gazing on visions of ecstasy :
The hue of his cheek and lip decay'd,
Around his mouth a sweet smile play'd ;—
　They look'd—he was dead !
　His spirit was fled :
Painless and swift as his own desire,
　The soul undress'd
　From her mortal rest
And stepp'd in her car of heavenly fire ;
　And proved how bright
　Were the realms of light,
Bursting at once upon the sight.
　　　　　　　James Edmeston

CXXXV

A DEATH SCENE

Dying, still slowly dying,
　As the hours of night rode by,
She had lain since the light of sunset
　Was red on the evening sky :
Till after the middle watches,
　As we softly near her trod,
When her soul from its prison fetters
　Was loosed by the hand of God.

One moment her pale lips trembled
　　With the triumph she might not tell,
As the sight of the life immortal
　　On her spirit's vision fell ;
Then the look of rapture faded,
　　And the beautiful smile was faint,
As that, in some convent picture,
　　On the face of a dying saint.

And we felt in the lonesome midnight,
　　As we sat by the silent dead,
What a light on the path going downward
　　The feet of the righteous shed.
Then we thought how, with faith unshrinking,
　　She came to the Jordan's tide,
And, taking the hand of the Saviour,
　　Went up on the heavenly side.
　　　　　　　　　Phœbe Carey

CXXXVI

THE DYING CHRISTIAN TO HIS SOUL

Vital spark of heavenly flame !
Quit, O quit this mortal frame :
Trembling, hoping, lingering, flying,
O, the pain, the bliss of dying !
Cease, fond Nature, cease thy strife,
And let me languish into life.

Hark! they whisper; Angels say,
Sister spirit, come away.
What is this absorbs me quite?
Steals my senses, shuts my sight,
Drowns my spirit, draws my breath?
Tell me, my soul, can this be death?

The world recedes, it disappears!
Heaven opens on my eyes! my ears
  With sounds seraphic ring:
Lend, lend your wings! I mount! I fly!
O grave! where is thy victory?
O death! where is thy sting?
A. Pope

CXXXVII

THE REAPER AND THE FLOWERS

There is a Reaper, whose name is Death,
  And, with his sickle keen,
He reaps the bearded grain at a breath,
  And the flowers that grow between.

"Shall I have nought that is fair?" saith he;
" Have nought but the bearded grain?
Though the breath of these flowers is sweet to me,
  I will give them all back again."

He gazed at the flowers with tearful eyes,
  He kiss'd their drooping leaves,
It was for the Lord of Paradise
  He bound them in his sheaves.

"My Lord has need of these flow'rets gay,"
　　The Reaper said, and smiled;
" Dear tokens of the earth are they,
　　Where He was once a child.

"They shall all bloom in fields of light,
　　Transplanted by my care,
And saints, upon their garments white,
　　These sacred blossoms wear."

And the mother gave, in tears and pain,
　　The flowers she most did love;
She knew she should find them all again
　　In the fields of light above.

O, not in cruelty, not in wrath,
　　The Reaper came that day;
'Twas an angel visited the green earth,
　　And took the flowers away.
　　　　　　　　　　H. W. Longfellow

CXXXVIII

ON THE DEATH OF A FAIR INFANT

O, fairest flower! no sooner blown but blasted,
Soft silken primrose fading timelessly,
Summer's chief honour, if thou had'st outlasted
Bleak winter's force that made thy blossom dry;
For he, being amorous of that lovely dye
　　That did thy cheek envermeil, sought to kiss,
But kill'd, alas! and then bewail'd his fatal bliss.

Yet can I not persuade me thou art dead,
Or that thy corse corrupts in earth's dark womb,
Or that thy beauties lie in wormy bed,
Hid from the world in a low delvèd tomb;
Could Heaven for pity thee so strictly doom?
　O no, for something in thy face did shine
Above mortality, that show'd thou wast divine.

O! wert thou of the golden wingèd host,
Who having clad thyself in human weed
To earth, from thy prefixèd seat didst post,
And after short abode fly back with speed,
As if to show what creatures Heaven doth breed;
　Thereby to set the hearts of men on fire
To scorn the sordid world, and unto Heaven aspire?

Then thou the mother of so sweet a child,
Her false imagin'd loss cease to lament,
And wisely learn to curb thy sorrows wild;
Think what a present thou to God hast sent,
And render Him with patience what He lent:
　This if thou do, He will an offering give,
That till the world's last end shall make thy name
　　to live.

J. Milton

CXXXIX
FUNERAL HYMN

Thou art gone to the grave! but we will not deplore
　thee,
Though sorrows and darkness encompass the tomb,
The Saviour hath past through its portal before
　thee,
And the lamp of His love is thy guide through
　the gloom.

Thou art gone to the grave! we no longer behold
    thee,
Nor tread the rough path of the world by thy side;
But the wide arms of mercy are spread to enfold
    thee,
And sinners may hope, since the Sinless has died.

Thou art gone to the grave! and, its mansion forsaking,
Perchance thy weak spirit in doubt linger'd long;
But the sunshine of Heav'n beam'd bright on thy
    waking,
And the sound which thou heard'st was the Seraphim's song.

Thou art gone to the grave! but 'twere vain to
    deplore thee,
When God was thy ransom, thy Guardian, and
    Guide;
He gave thee, He took thee, and He will restore
    thee,
And death hath no sting, since the Saviour has died.
            Bishop Heber

CXL

THE BURIAL ANTHEM

Brother, thou art gone before us,
  And thy saintly soul is flown
Where tears are wiped from every eye,
  And sorrow is unknown.

From the burden of the flesh,
    And from care and sin releas'd,
Where the wicked cease from troubling,
    And the weary are at rest.

The toilsome way thou'st travell'd o'er,
    And borne the heavy load;
But Christ hath taught thy languid feet
    To reach His blest abode;
Thou'rt sleeping now, like Lazarus,
    Upon his Father's breast,
Where the wicked cease from troubling,
    And the weary are at rest.

Sin can never taint thee now,
    Nor doubt thy faith assail,
Nor thy meek trust in Jesus Christ
    And the Holy Spirit fail;
And there thou'rt sure to meet the good,
    Whom on earth thou lovedst best,
Where the wicked cease from troubling,
    And the weary are at rest.

"Earth to earth," and "dust to dust,"
    The solemn Priest hath said;
So we lay the turf above thee now,
    And we seal thy narrow bed:
But thy spirit, brother, soars away
    Among the faithful blest,
Where the wicked cease from troubling,
    And the weary are at rest.

And when the Lord shall summon us
  Whom thou hast left behind,
May we, untainted by the world,
  As sure a welcome find ;
May each, like thee, depart in peace,
  To be a glorious guest,
Where the wicked cease from troubling,
  And the weary are at rest.

H. H. Milman

CXLI

AN EPITAPH

Receive him, earth, unto thine harbouring shrine ;
  In thy soft tranquil bosom let him rest ;
These limbs of man I to thy care consign,
  And trust the noble fragments to thy breast.

This house was once the mansion of a soul
  Brought into life by its Creator's breath ;
Wisdom did once this living mass control ;
  And Christ was there enshrined, who conquers death.

Cover this body to thy care consign'd ;
  Its Maker shall not leave it in the grave ;
But His own lineaments shall bear in mind,
  And shall recall the image which He gave.

I. Williams,
from Prudentius

CXLII
FEAR OF DEATH

O miserable man,
Who hath all the world to friend,
Yet dares not in prosperity
Remember his latter end!

But happy man, whate'er
  His earthly lot may be,
Who looks on death as the angel
  That shall set his spirit free,
  And bear it to his heritage
    Of immortality.
            R. Southey

CXLIII
'ALL SAINTS' DAY
The gathering of the Dead

The day is cloudy; it should be so:
And the clouds in flocks to the eastward go;
For the world may not see the glory there,
Where Christ and His Saints are met in the air.
There is a stir among all things round,
Like the shock of an earthquake underground,
And there is music in the motion,
As soft and deep as a summer ocean.
All things that sleep awake to-day,

For the cross and the crown are won,
    The winds of spring
    Sweet songs may bring
Through the half-unfolded leaves of May;
    But the breeze of spring
    Hath no such thing
As the musical sounds that run
Where the anthem note by God is given,
    And the martyrs sing,
    And the angels ring
With the cymbals of highest Heaven.
In Heaven above, and on earth beneath,
   In the holy place where dead men sleep,
In the silent sepulchres of death,
   Where angels over the bodies keep
Their cheerful watch till the second breath
   Into the Christian dust shall creep—
In heights, and depths, and darkest caves,
In the unlit green of the ocean waves—
In fields where battles have been fought,
Dungeons where murders have been wrought—
The shock and the thrill of life have run :
The reign of the Holy is begun !
There is labour and unquietness
In the very sands of the wilderness,
    In the place where rivers ran.
Where the simoon blast hath fiercely past,
    O'er the midnight caravan.
From sea to sea, from shore to shore,
Earth travails with her dead once more.
In one long, endless, filing crowd,
    Apostles, Martyrs, Saints have gone,
Where behind yon screen of cloud

The Master is upon His throne!
Only we are left alone!
Left in this waste and desert place,
  Far from our natural home;
Left to complete our weary race
  Until His kingdom come.
O, my God! that we could be
Among that shining company!
But once a year with solemn hand
  The Church withdraws the veil,
And there we see that other land,
  Far in the distance pale.
While good church bells are loudly ringing
  All on the earth below,
And white-robed choirs with angels singing,
  Where stately organs blow:
And up and down each holy street
Faith hears the tread of viewless feet,
Such as in Salem walk'd, when He
Had gotten Himself the victory.
So be it ever year by year,
Until the Judge himself be here!
                    F. W. Faber

CXLIV

EPITAPH IN WORCESTER CATHEDRAL

If Heavenly flowers might bloom unharm'd on
    earth,
  And gales of Eden still their balm bestow,
Thy gentle virtues rich in purest worth,
  Might yet have linger'd in our vale below;

Loved daughter, sister, friend : we saw awhile
    Thy meek-eyed modesty which loved the shade,
Thy faithfulness which knew nor change, nor guile,
    Thy heart like incense on God's altar laid.

But He whose spirit breathes the air divine,
    That gives to souls their loveliness and grace,
Soonest embowers pure faithful hearts like thine
    In His own Paradise, their blissful place.
John Davison

CXLV

THE HAPPY DEAD

'Tis folly all that can be said,
By living mortals, of the immortal dead.
    'Tis as if we who stay behind
    In expectation of the wind,
Should pity those who pass'd this strait before
    And touch the universal shore.
Ah, happy man, who art to sail no more !
A. Cowley

CXLVI

EPITAPH UPON HUSBAND AND WIFE
Who died and were buried together

To these, whom death again did wed,
This grave's the second marriage bed,
For though the hand of fate could force
'Twixt soul and body a divorce,
It could not sever man and wife,
Because they both lived but one life.

Peace, good reader, do not weep,
Peace, the lovers are asleep!
They (sweet turtles) folded lie,
In the last knot love could tie.
Let them sleep, let them sleep on,
Till this stormy night be gone,
And the eternal morrow dawn;
Then the curtains will be drawn,
And they wake into a light,
Whose day shall never end in night.
                              R. Crashaw

CXLVII
ELEGY ON THE DEATH OF ADDISON

What mourner ever felt poetic fires?
Slow comes the verse that real love inspires:
Grief unaffected suits but ill with art,
Or flowing numbers with a bleeding heart.
Can I forget the dismal night that gave
My soul's best part for ever to the grave!
How silent did his old companions tread!
By midnight lamps the mansions of the dead;
Through breathing statues, then unheeded things,
Through rows of warriors, and through walks o
    kings!
What awe did the slow solemn knell inspire;
The pealing organ, and the pausing choir;
The duties by the lawn-rob'd prelate paid;
And the last words that dust to dust convey'd!
While speechless o'er thy closing grave we bend,
Accept these tears thou dear departed friend.

O, gone for ever ! take this long adieu ;
And sleep in peace next thy lov'd Montague.
Oft let me range the gloomy aisles alone,
Sad luxury to vulgar minds unknown,
Along the walls, where speaking marbles show
What worthies form the hallow'd mould below
Proud names, who once the reins of empire held
In arms who triumph'd ; or in arts excell'd ;
Chiefs grand with scars, and prodigal of blood ;
Stern patriots who for sacred freedom stood.
Just men by whom imperial laws were given,
And saints who taught, and led the way to heaven ;
Ne'er to these chambers where the mighty rest,
Since their foundation, came a nobler guest ;
Nor e'er was to the bowers of bliss convey'd
A fairer spirit, or more welcome shade.
Tickell

CXLVIII

SUSPIRIA

Take them, O Death ! and bear away
    Whatever thou canst call thine own !
Thine image, stamp'd upon this clay,
    Doth give thee that, but that alone !

Take them, O Grave ! and let them lie
    Folded upon thy narrow shelves,
As garments by the soul laid by,
    And precious only to ourselves !

Take them, O great Eternity !
    Our little life is but a gust,
That bends the branches of thy tree,
    And trails its blossoms in the dust !
H. W. Longfellow

CXLIX

LADY MARY

Thou wert fair, Lady Mary,
    As the lily in the sun;
And fairer yet thou mightest be—
    Thy youth was but begun:
Thine eye was soft and glancing,
    Of the deep bright blue;
And on the heart thy gentle words
    Fell lighter than the dew.

They found thee, Lady Mary,
    With thy palms upon thy breast,
Even as thou hadst been praying
    At thy hour of rest:
The cold pale moon was shining
    On thy cold pale cheek;
And the morn of the Nativity
    Had just begun to break.

They carved thee, Lady Mary,
    All of pure white stone,
With thy palms upon thy breast,
    In the chancel all alone:
And I saw thee when the winter moon
    Play'd on thy marble cheek,
When the morn of the Nativity
    Had just begun to break.

But thou kneelest, Lady Mary,
   With thy palms upon thy breast,
Among the perfect spirits
   In the land of rest :
Thou art even as they took thee
   At thine hour of prayer,
Save the glory that is on thee
   From the Sun that shineth there.

We shall see thee, Lady Mary,
   On that shore unknown,
A pure and happy angel
   In the presence of the Throne ;
We shall see thee when the light Divine
   Plays freshly on thy cheek,
And the Resurrection morning
   Hath just begun to break.

H. Alford

CL

MY BROTHER'S GRAVE

Beneath the chancel's hallow'd stone,
   Exposed to every rustic tread—
To few, save rustic mourners known,—
   My brother, is thy lowly bed.
Few words upon the rough stone graven
   Thy name, thy birth, thy youth declare—
Thy innocence, thy hopes of Heaven—
   In simplest phrase recorded there :
No scutcheons shine, no banners wave
In mockery o'er my brother's grave.

The place is silent—rarely sound
Is heard those ancient walls around;
Nor mirthful voice of friends that meet
Discoursing in the public street,
Nor hum of business dull and loud,
Nor murmur of the passing crowd,
Nor soldier's drum, nor trumpet's swell
From neighbouring fort, or citadel,—
No sound of human toil, or strife,
To death's lone dwelling speaks of life;
Nor breaks the silence still and deep,
  Where thou, beneath thy burial stone,
Art laid in that unbroken sleep,
  The living eye hath never known.
The lonely sexton's footstep falls
In dismal echoes on the walls,
As slowly pacing through the aisle,
  He sweeps the unholy dust away,
And cobwebs, which must not defile
  Those windows on the Sabbath day;
And, passing through the central nave,
Treads lightly on my brother's grave.

But when the sweet-toned Sabbath chime,
  Pouring its music on the breeze,
Proclaims the well-known holy time
  Of prayer, and thanks, and bended knees—
When rustic crowds devoutly meet,
  And lips and hearts to God are given,
And souls enjoy oblivion sweet
  Of earthly ills in hope of Heaven;—
What voice of calm and solemn tone
Is heard above thy burial stone?

What form in priestly meek array,
Beside the altar kneels to pray?
What holy hands are lifted up
To bless the sacramental cup?
Full well I know that reverend form;
   And, if a voice could reach the dead,
Those tones would reach thee, though the worm
   My brother made thy heart his bed;
That sire, who thy existence gave,
Now stands beside thy lowly grave.

It is not long since thou wert wont
   Within these sacred walls to kneel;
This altar, that baptismal font,
   These stones which now thy dust conceal,
The sweet tones of the Sabbath bell,
   Were holiest objects to thy soul;
On these thy spirit loved to dwell
   Untainted by the world's control.
My brother, those were happy days
   When thou and I were children yet;
How fondly memory still surveys
   Those scenes the heart can ne'er forget!
My soul was then, as thine is now,
   Unstain'd by sin, unstung by pain;
Peace smiled on each unclouded brow—
   Mine ne'er will be so calm again.
How blithely then we hail'd the ray
Which usher'd in the Sabbath day!
How lightly then our footsteps trod
Yon pathway to the house of God!
For souls in which no dark offence
Hath sullied childhood's innocence,

Best meet the pure and hallow'd shrine,
Which guiltier bosoms own Divine.
I feel not now as then I felt—
　The sunshine of my heart is o'er;
The spirit now is changed, which dwelt
　Within me in the days before;
But thou wert snatch'd; my brother, hence
In all thy guileless innocence.
One Sabbath saw thee bend thy knee
In reverential piety,
For childish faults forgiveness crave,—
The next beamed brightly on thy grave.
The crowd, of which thou late wert one,
Now throng'd across thy burial stone;
Rude footsteps trampled on the spot
Where thou liest mouldering and forgot;
And some few gentler bosoms wept
In silence where my brother slept.

And years have pass'd, and thou art now
　Forgotten in thy silent tomb;
And cheerful is my mother's brow,
　My father's eye has lost its gloom;
And years have pass'd, and death has laid
　Another victim at thy side;
With thee he roams, an infant shade,
　But not more pure than thou he died.
Blest are ye both! your ashes rest
Beside the spot ye loved the best;
And that dear home which saw your birth
O'erlooks you in your bed of earth;
But who can tell what blissful shore
Your angel spirits wander o'er?

And who can tell what raptures high
Now bless your immortality?
My boyish days are nearly gone,
   My breast is not unsullied now;
And worldly cares and woes will soon
   Cut their deep furrows on my brow;
And life will take a darker hue
From ills my brother never knew.
And I have made me bosom friends,
   And lov'd, and link'd my heart with others;
But who with mine his spirit blends
   As mine was blended with my brother's?
When years of rapture glided by,
   The spring of life's unclouded weather,
Our souls were knit, and thou, and I,
   My brother, grew in love together;
The chain is broke which bound us then—
Where shall I find its like again?

J. Moultrie

CLI

A WALK IN A CHURCHYARD

We walk'd within the churchyard bounds,
   My little boy, and I—
He, laughing, running happy rounds,
   I, pacing mournfully.

"Nay, child, it is not well," I said,
   "Among the graves to shout;
To laugh and play among the dead,
   And make this noisy rout."

A moment to my side he clung,
  Leaving his merry play,—
A moment still'd his joyous tongue,
  Almost as hush'd as they.

Then, quite forgetting the command,
  In life's exulting burst
Of early glee, let go my hand,
  Joyous, as at the first.

And now I did not check him more;
  For, taught by Nature's face,
I had grown wiser than before,
  Even in that moment's space.

She spread no funeral pall above
  That patch of churchyard ground,
But the same azure vault of love
  As hung o'er all around.

And white clouds o'er that spot would pass
  As freely as elsewhere;
The sunshine on no other grass
  A richer hue might wear.

And, form'd from out that very mould
  In which the dead did lie,
The daisy with its eye of gold
  Look'd up into the sky.

The rook was wheeling over head,
  Nor hasten'd to be gone;
The small bird did its glad notes shed,
  Perch'd on a grey head stone.

And God, I said, would never give
   This light upon the earth ;
Nor bid in childhood's heart to live,
   These springs of gushing mirth ;

If our true wisdom were to mourn
   And linger with the dead,—
To nurse, as wisest, thoughts forlorn
   Of worm, and earthy bed.

Oh ! no, the glory earth puts on,
   The child's uncheck'd delight,
Both witness to a triumph won,
   If we but judge aright.

A triumph won o'er sin and death :
   From these the Saviour saves ;
And like a happy infant, Faith
   Can play among the graves.
                    Archbishop Trench

CLII
ON MY MOTHER'S PICTURE

Oh that those lips had language ! Life has pass'd
With me but roughly since I heard thee last :
Those lips are thine—thine own sweet smile I see,
The same, that oft in childhood solac'd me ;
Voice only fails, else how distinct they say,
" Grieve not, my child, chase all thy fears away !"
The meek intelligence of those dear eyes
(Blest be the art that can immortalize—
The art that baffles Time's tyrannic claim
To quench it) here shines on me still the same.

Faithful remembrancer of one so dear,
O welcome guest, though unexpected here!
Who bidd'st me honour with an artless song,
Affectionate, a mother lost so long,
I will obey, not willingly alone,
But gladly, as the precept were her own:
And, while that face renews my filial grief,
Fancy shall weave a charm for my relief,
Shall steep me in Elysian reverie,
A momentary dream, that thou art she.
My mother! when I learn'd that thou wast dead,
Say, wast thou conscious of the tears I shed?
Hover'd thy spirit o'er thy sorrowing son,
Wretch even then, Life's journey just begun?
Perhaps thou gav'st me, though unfelt, a kiss;
Perhaps a tear, if souls can weep in bliss—
Ah, that maternal smile! it answers—Yes.
I heard the bell toll'd on thy burial day,
I saw the hearse that bore thee slow away,
And, turning from my nurs'ry window, drew
A long, long sigh, and wept a last adieu!
But was it such?—It was. Where thou art gone
Adieus and farewells are a sound unknown:
May I but meet thee on that peaceful shore,
The parting word shall pass my lips no more!
Thy maidens, griev'd themselves at my concern,
Oft gave me promise of thy quick return.
What ardently I wish'd, I long believ'd,
And, disappointed still, was still deceiv'd.
By expectation ev'ry day beguil'd,
Dupe of *to-morrow* even from a child.
Thus many a sad to-morrow came and went,
Till, all my stock of infant sorrow spent,

I learn'd at last submission to my lot;
But, though I less deplor'd thee, ne'er forgot.
Where once we dwelt, our name is heard no more—
Children not thine have trod my nurs'ry floor;
And where the gard'ner, Robin, day by day,
Drew me to school along the public way,
Delighted with my bauble coach, and wrapp'd
In scarlet mantle warm, and velvet capp'd,
'Tis now become a hist'ry little known,
That once we called the past'ral house our own.
Shortliv'd possession! but the record fair,
That mem'ry keeps of all thy kindness there,
Still outlives many a storm that has effac'd
A thousand other themes less deeply trac'd.
Thy nightly visits to my chamber made,
That thou might'st know me safe, and warmly laid;
Thy morning bounties ere I left my home—
The biscuit, or confectionary plum;
The fragrant waters on my cheeks bestow'd
By thy own hand, till fresh they shone, and glow'd;
All this, and more endearing still than all,
Thy constant flow of love, that knew no fall,
Ne'er roughen'd by those cataracts and breaks
That humour interpos'd too often makes;
All this, still legible in mem'ry's page,
And still to be so to my latest age,
Adds joy to duty, makes me glad to pay
Such honours to thee as my numbers may;
Perhaps a frail memorial, but sincere—
Not scorn'd in Heav'n, though little notic'd here.
Could Time, his flight revers'd, restore the hours,
When, playing with thy vesture's tissued flowers,
The violet, the pink, and jessamine,

I prick'd them into paper with a pin,
(And thou wast happier than myself the while—
Would'st softly speak, and stroke my head, and smile)—
Could those few pleasant days again appear,
Might one wish bring them, would I wish them here?
I would not trust my heart—the dear delight
Seems so to be desir'd, perhaps I might.
But no—what here we call our life is such,
So little to be lov'd, and thou so much,
That I should ill requite thee to constrain
Thy unbound spirit into bonds again.
Thou—as a gallant bark from Albion's coast
(The storms all weather'd and the ocean crossed)
Shoots into port at some well-haven'd isle,
Where spices breathe, and brighter seasons smile,
There sits quiescent on the floods that shew
Her beauteous form reflected clear below,
While airs impregnated with incense play
Around her, fanning light her streamers gay ;—
So thou, with sails how swift! hast reach'd the shore
"Where tempests never beat, nor billows roar,"
And thy lov'd consort on the dang'rous tide
Of life, long since has anchor'd by thy side.
But me, scarce hoping to obtain that rest,
Always from port withheld, always distrest—
Me, howling blasts drive devious, tempest-toss'd,
Sails ripp'd, seams op'ning wide, and compass lost,
And day by day some current's thwarting force
Sets me more distant from a prosp'rous course.
Yet O the thought, that thou art safe, and he !
That thought is joy, arrive what may to me.

My boast is not that I deduce my birth
From loins enthron'd, and rulers of the earth ;
But higher far my proud pretensions rise—
The son of parents pass'd into the skies.
And now farewell—Time unrevok'd has run
His wonted course, yet what I wish'd is done.
By contemplation's help, not sought in vain,
I seem t' have liv'd my childhood o'er again ;
To have renewed the joys that once were mine
Without the sin of violating thine ;
And, while the wings of Fancy still are free,
And I can view this mimic show of thee,
Time has but half-succeeded in his theft—
Thyself remov'd, thy power to soothe me left.
W. Cowper.

CLIII

PRINCE ALBERT

   We have lost him ; he is gone !
We know him now : all narrow jealousies
Are silent ; and we see him as he moved :
How modest, kindly, all-accomplish'd, wise,
With what sublime repression of himself,
And in what limits, and how tenderly ;
Not swaying to this faction, or to that ;
Not making his high place the lawless perch
Of wing'd ambition, nor a vantage ground
For pleasure ; but through all this tract of years
Wearing the white flower of a blameless life,
Before a thousand peering littlenesses,
In that fierce light which beats upon a throne,

And blackens every blot : for where is he,
Who dares foreshadow for an only son
A lovelier life, a more unstain'd, than his?
Or how should England, dreaming of his sons,
Hope more for these than some inheritance
Of such a life, a heart, a mind as thine,
Thou noble Father of her kings to be !
Laborious for her people, and her poor—
Voice in the rich dawn of an ampler day—
Far-sighted summoner of War and Waste
To fruitful strifes, and rivalries of peace—
Sweet nature, gilded by the gracious gleam
Of letters dear to Science, dear to Art,
Dear to thy land and ours, a Prince indeed,
Beyond all titles, and a household name
Hereafter, through all time, Albert the Good!

Break not, O woman's heart, but still endure ;
Break not, for thou art Royal, but endure,
Remembering all the beauty of that star
Which shone so close beside thee, that ye made
One light together, but has past, and leaves
The crown a lonely splendour.

May all love,
His love unseen but felt, o'ershadow thee,
The love of all thy sons encompass thee,
The love of all thy daughters cherish thee,
The love of all thy people comfort thee,
Till God's love set thee at his side again.
A. Tennyson

CLIV

FIRE

Sweet maiden, for so calm a life
  Too bitter seem'd thy end ;
But thou hadst won thee, ere that strife
  A more than earthly Friend.

We miss thee in thy place at school,
  And in thine homeward way,
Where violets, by the reedy pool
  Peep out so shyly gay ;

Where thou, a true and gentle guide,
  Wouldst lead thy little band,
With all an elder sister's pride,
  And rule with heart and hand.

And if we miss, O who may speak
  What thoughts are hovering round
The pallet where thy fresh young cheek
  Its evening slumber found ?

How many a tearful, longing look,
  In silence seeks thee yet,
Where in its own familiar nook
  Thy fireside chair is set.

And oft, when little voices dim,
  Are feeling for the note,
In chanted prayer, or psalm, or hymn,
  And, wavering, wildly float,

Comes gushing o'er a sudden thought
  Of her who led the strain,
How oft such music home she brought—
  But ne'er shall bring again.

O, say not so! the spring-tide air
  Is fraught with whisperings sweet ;
Who knows but heavenly carols there
  With ours may duly meet ?

Who knows how near, each holy hour,
  The pure and child-like dead
May linger, when in shrine or bower
  The mourner's prayer is said?

And He who will'd thy tender frame
  (O, stern but sweet decree !)
Should wear the martyr's robe of flame—
  He hath prepar'd for thee

A garland in that region bright
  Where infant spirits reign,
Ting'd faintly with such golden light
  As crowns His martyr train.

Nay, doubt it not : His tokens sure
  Were round her death-bed shown :
The wasting pain might not endure,
  'Twas calm ere life had flown ;

Even as we read of saints of yore :
  Her heart and voice were free
To crave one quiet slumber more
  Upon her mother's knee.

J. Keble

CLV

FOOTSTEPS OF ANGELS

When the hours of Day are number'd,
    And the voices of the Night
Wake the better soul, that slumber'd,
    In a holy, calm delight;

Ere the evening lamps are lighted,
    And, like phantoms grim and tall,
Shadows from the fitful fire-light
    Dance upon the parlour wall;

Then the forms of the departed
    Enter at the open door;
The belovèd, the true-hearted,
    Come to visit me once more;

He, the young and strong, who cherish'd
    Noble longings for the strife,
By the road-side fell and perish'd,
    Weary with the march of life!

They, the holy ones and weakly,
    Who the cross of suffering bore,
Folded their pale hands so meekly,
    Spake with us on earth no more!

And with them the Being Beauteous,
    Who unto my youth was given,
More than all things else to love me,
    And is now a saint in Heaven.

With a slow and noiseless footstep
  Comes that messenger divine,
Takes the vacant chair beside me,
  Lays her gentle hand in mine.

And she sits and gazes at me
  With those deep and tender eyes,
Like the stars, so still and saintlike,
  Looking downward from the skies.

Utter'd not, yet comprehended
  Is the spirit's voiceless prayer,
Soft rebukes, in blessings ended,
  Breathing from her lips of air.

O, though oft depress'd and lonely,
  All my fears are laid aside,
If I but remember only
  Such as these have lived, and died!
                H. W. Longfellow

CLVI

RESIGNATION

There is no flock, however watch'd and tended,
  But one dead lamb is there!
There is no fireside, howsoe'er defended,
  But has one vacant chair.

The air is full of farewells to the dying,
  And mournings for the dead;
The heart of Rachel, for her children crying,
  Will not be comforted!

Let us be patient! These severe afflictions
  Not from the ground arise,
But oftentimes celestial benedictions
  Assume this dark disguise.

We see but dimly through the mists and vapours;
  Amid these earthly damps;
What seem to us but sad, funereal tapers,
  May be Heaven's distant lamps.

There is no Death! What seems so is transition;
  This life of mortal breath
Is but a suburb of the life Elysian,
  Whose portal we call Death.

She is not dead,—the child of our affection,—
  But gone unto that school
Where she no longer needs our poor protection,
  And Christ Himself doth rule.

In that great cloister's stillness and seclusion,
  By guardian angels led,
Safe from temptation, safe from sin's pollution,
  She lives, whom we call dead.

Day after day, we think what she is doing
  In those bright realms of air:
Year after year, her tender steps pursuing,
  Behold her grown more fair.

Thus do we walk with her, and keep unbroken
  The bond which nature gives,
Thinking that our remembrance, though unspoken,
  May reach her where she lives.

Not as a child shall we again behold her;
 For, when with raptures wild,
In our embraces we again enfold her,
 She will not be a child;

But a fair maiden in her Father's mansion,
 Cloth'd with celestial grace;
And beautiful with all the soul's expansion
 Shall we behold her face.

And though at times impetuous with emotion
 And anguish long suppress'd,
The swelling heart heaves moaning like the ocean
 That cannot be at rest,—

We will be patient, and assuage the feeling
 We may not wholly stay;
By silence sanctifying, not concealing,
 The grief that must have way.

H. W. Longfellow

CLVII

GENOVEVA

Gently speak, and lightly tread,
'Tis the chamber of the dead.
Now thine earthly course is run,
Now thy weary day is done,
Genoveva, sainted one!

Happy flight thy sprite has taken,
From its plumes earth's last dust shaken:
On the earth is passionate weeping,
Round thy bier lone vigils keeping,—
In the heaven triumphant songs,
Welcome of angelic throngs,

As thou enterest on that day
Which no tears, nor fears allay,
No regrets, nor pangs affray,
Hemm'd not in by yesterday,
By to-morrow hemm'd not in,
Weep not for her—she doth win
What we long for ; now is she
That which all desire to be.
Bear her forth with solemn cheer,
Bear her forth on open bier,
That the wonder which hath been
May of every eye be seen.
Wonderful! that pale worn brow
Death hath scarcely seal'd, and now
All the beauty that she wore
In the youthful years before,
All the freshness, and the grace,
And the bloom upon her face,
Ere that seven year'd distress
In the painful wilderness,
Ere that wasting sickness came,
Undermining quite her frame,
All come back—the light, the hue,
Tinge her cheek and lip anew :
Far from her, oh ! far away
All that is so quick to say
" Man returneth to his clay ;"
All that to our creeping fear
Whispers of corruption near.
Seems it as she would illume,
With her radiance and her bloom,
The dark spaces of the tomb.

Archbishop Trench

CLVIII
DEATH OF A CHRISTIAN

Calm on the bosom of thy God,
  Fair spirit, rest thee now!
E'en while with ours thy footsteps trod
  His seal was on thy brow.

Dust, to its narrow house beneath!
  Soul, to its place on high!
They, that have seen thy look in death,
  No more may fear to die.
Mrs. Hemans

CLIX
THE CHURCH OF BERN
The Tomb

So rest, for ever rest, O Princely Pair!
In your high church, 'mid the still mountain air,
Where horn, and hound, and vassals, never come,
Only the blessed Saints are smiling dumb
From the rich painted windows of the nave
On aisle, and transept, and your marble grave;
Where thou, young Prince, shalt never more arise
From the fring'd mattress where thy Duchess lies,
On Autumn mornings, when the bugle sounds,
And ride across the drawbridge with thy hounds
To hunt the boar in the crisp woods till eve.
And thou, O Princess, shalt no more receive,
Thou and thy ladies in the hall of state,
The jaded hunters with their bloody freight,
Coming benighted to the castle gate.

The Sunday

So sleep, for ever sleep, O Marble Pair!
And if ye wake, let it be then, when fair,
On the carv'd western front, a flood of light
Streams from the setting sun, and colours bright
Prophets, transfigur'd saints, and martyrs brave,
In the vast western window of the nave;
And on the pavement round the tomb there glints
A chequer-work of glowing sapphire tints,
And amethyst, and ruby;—then unclose
Your eyelids on the stone where ye repose,
And from your broider'd pillows lift your heads,
And rise upon your cold white marble beds,
And looking down on the warm rosy tints
That chequer, at your feet, the illumin'd flints,
Say—" What is this? we are in bliss—forgiven—
Behold the pavement of the courts of Heaven!"—
Or let it be on Autumn nights, when rain
Doth rustlingly above your heads complain
On the smooth leaden roof; and on the walls,
Shedding her pensive light at intervals,
The moon through the clerestory windows shines;
And the wind washes in the mountain pines.
Then gazing up through the dim pillars high,
The foliag'd marble forest where ye lie,
"Hush!" ye will say—"it is eternity!
This is the glimmering verge of Heaven, and these
The columns of the Heavenly Palaces."
And in the sweeping of the wind your ear
The passage of the Angels' wings will hear,
And on the lichen-crusted leads above
The rustle of the eternal rain of Love.

Matthew Arnold

CLX
LONGING FOR HOME

A song of a boat :—
There was once a boat on a billow :
Lightly she rock'd to her port remote,
And the foam was white in her wake like snow,
And her frail mast bow'd when the breeze would
    blow,
And bent like a wand of willow.

I shaded mine eyes one day when a boat
    Went curtseying over the billow ;
I mark'd her course till, a dancing mote,
She faded out on the moonlit foam,
And I stay'd behind in the dear-lov'd home :
    And my thoughts all day were about the boat,
    And my dreams upon the pillow.

I pray you hear my song of a boat,
    For it is but short :—
My boat, you shall find none fairer afloat
    In river or port.
Long I look'd out for the lad she bore
    On the open desolate sea,
And I think he sail'd to the heavenly shore,
    For he came not back to me.

A song of a nest :—
There was once a nest in a hollow,
Down in the mosses and knot-grass press'd
    Soft, and warm, and full to the brim ;
    Vetches lean'd over it purple and dim,
With buttercup buds to follow.

I pray you hear my song of a nest,
  For it is not long :—
You shall never light in a summer quest
  The bushes among—
Shall never light on a prouder litter,
  A fairer nestful, nor ever know
A softer sound than their tender twitter,
  That wind-like did come and go.

I had a nestful once of my own,
  Ah happy, happy I!
Right dearly I lov'd them: but when they were grown
  They spread out their wings to fly—
O, one after one they flew away
  Far up to the heavenly blue,
To the better country, the upper day,
  And—I wish I was going too.

I pray you, what is the nest to me—
  My empty nest?
And what is the shore where I stood to see
  My boat sail down to the west?
Can I call that home where I anchor yet,
  Though my good man has sail'd?
Can I call that home where my heart was set
  Now all its hope has failed?
Nay, but the port where my sailor went,
  And the land where my nestlings be;
There is the home where my hopes are sent,
  The only home for me.

J. Ingelow

CLXI

STRIFE AND PEACE

The yellow poplar leaves came down
    And like a carpet lay,
No waftings were in the sunny air
    To flutter them away;
And he stepp'd on blithe and debonnair,
    That warm October day.

" The boy," saith he, " hath got his own,
    But sore has been the fight,
For ere his life began the strife
    That ceas'd but yesternight;
For the will," he said, " the kinsfolk read,
    And read it not aright.

" His cause was argued in the court
    Before his christening day,
And counsel was heard, and judge demurr'd,
    And bitter wax'd the fray;
Brother with brother spake no word
    When they met in the way.

" Against each one did each contend,
    And all against the heir,
I would not bend, for I knew the end—
    I have it for my share,
And nought repent, though my best friend
    From henceforth I must spare.

"Manor, and moor, and farm, and wold,
  Their greed begrudg'd him sore,
And parchments old with passionate hold
  They guarded heretofore;
And they carp'd at signature and seal,
  But they may carp no more.

"An old affront will stir the heart
  Thro' years of rankling pain,
And I feel the fret that urged me yet
  That warfare to maintain;
For an enemy's loss may well be set
  Against an infant's gain.

"An enemy's loss I go to prove;
  Laugh out, thou little heir!
Laugh in his face, who vow'd to chase
  Thee from thy birthright fair;
For I come to set thee in thy place;
  Laugh out, and do not spare."

A man of strife, in wrathful mood
  He near'd the nurse's door;
With poplar leaves the roof and eaves
  Were thickly scatter'd o'er,
And yellow as they, a sunbeam lay
  Along the cottage floor.

"Sleep on, thou pretty, pretty lamb,"
  He hears the fond nurse say;
"And if angels stand at thy right hand,
  As now belike they may,
And if angels meet at thy bed's feet,
  I fear them not this day.

"Come wealth, come want to thee, dear heart,
   It was all one to me,
For thy pretty tongue far sweeter rung,
   Than coinèd gold and fee,
And ever the while thy waking smile
   It was right fair to see.

"Sleep, pretty bairn, and never know
   Who grudg'd and who transgress'd ;
Thee to retain, I was full fain,
   But God He knoweth best !
And His peace upon thy brow lies plain
   As the sunshine on thy breast."

The man of strife he enters in,
   Looks, and his pride doth cease ;
Anger and sorrow shall be to-morrow,
   Trouble, and no release ;
For the babe whose life awoke the strife
   Hath enter'd into peace.
                              J. Ingelow

CLXII

THE MOTHER'S DEATH

Methought I heard a sound, methought it came
From my poor mother's room—I softly crept
And listen'd : in the middle of the night
I heard her talk with God.—" Thou knowest well
That sorrow has been with me like a babe
In my great solitude, till I have come
To love its smileless face. Thou Love who wrapt

Thyself in flesh, and sat awhile disguised
At the rude feast of our humanity,
And tasted every sweet and bitter there,
Then rose, and unsuspected went away :
Who loved the humble ones at Bethany ;
Who wept o'er Lazarus, and with Thy tears
Comforted all the family of grief,
In every time, in every far-off land ;—
Thou infinite tenderness wilt pardon me
If my heart murmur'd when my lips were still.
Our life is noble, Thou hast breath'd its air ;
Death sweet, for Thou hast died. On Thy way
    home
One night Thou slept'st within the dreadful grave,
And took away its fear. O, smile on me !
The world and I have done ; with humble heart
I sit down at Thy glorious gates and wait
Till death shall lead me in. But chiefly bless
My poor boy, left alone in this ill world :
I never more may look upon his face,
May never hear his voice. Thou know'st him well,
For every morning, long before the lark
Sang at Thy shining doors, my prayer arose
To crave Thy blessing on his restless youth.
It is the evening of my day of life,
I have been working from the early dawn,
Am sore, and weary ; let me go to sleep,—
Let me stretch out my limbs, and be at rest
In the untroubled silence of the grave."
My heart swell'd like a man's who, after years
Wasted in riot 'neath a tropic sky,
Returns, and wandering on a Sabbath eve,
Bursts into tears beside a twilight church,

Fill'd with a psalm which he knew long ago
When his heart too was pure.
                        I ran to her,
But she had sunk in swoon, and there I stood
Like one too late upon a brink, who sees
The water closing over all he loves.
I knelt down by the bed. " Come, Margery !
The sea is glittering in the sunny bay,
The fisher's nets are drying on the shore,
And let us gather silver purple shells
For necklaces. You have been in the woods ;
Your lips are black with berries. O the boats !
The bonny bonny boats ! List, the fishers sing ! "
" O, mother, mother ! "

                " They have left me here,
Upon this dark and lonely, lonely road ;
I cannot hear a voice, or touch a hand ;
O Father, take me home !" She sobb'd and wept
As if she were a little wander'd child.
Her Father took her home, I stoop'd to catch
Her feeble breath, a change came o'er her look,
A flutter in her throat, and all was peace.
                            A. Smith

CLXIII

ON THE GRAVE OF BISHOP KEN, AT FROME, SOMERSETSHIRE

Let other thoughts, where'er I roam,
  Ne'er from my memory cancel
The coffin-fashion'd tomb at Frome,
  That lies behind the chancel ;

A basket-work where bars are bent,
   Iron in place of osier,
And shapes above that represent
   A mitre and a crosier.

These signs of him that slumbers there
   The dignity betoken;
These iron bars a heart declare
   Hard bent but never broken;
This form portrays how souls like his,
   Their pride and passion quelling,
Preferr'd to earth's high palaces
   This calm and narrow dwelling.

There with the churchyard's common dust
   He lov'd his own to mingle;
The faith in which he placed his trust
   Was nothing rare or single:
Yet laid he to the sacred wall
   As close as he was able,
The blessèd crumbs might almost fall
   Upon him from God's table.

Who was this father of the Church,
   So secret in his glory?
In vain might antiquarians search
   For record of his story;
But preciously tradition keeps
   The fame of holy men;
So there the Christian smiles or weeps
   For love of Bishop Ken.

A name his country once forsook,
  But now with joy inherits,
Confessor in the Church's book,
  And martyr in the Spirit's !
That dared with royal power to cope,
  In peaceful faith persisting,
A braver Becket—who could hope
  To conquer unresisting

R. M. Milnes

CLXIV

NEW-YEAR'S EVE

If you're waking, call me early, call me early, mother dear,
For I would see the sun rise upon the glad new-year.
It is the last new-year that I shall ever see,
Then you may lay me low i' the mould, and think no more of me.

To-night I saw the sun set : he set and left behind
The good old year, the dear old time, and all my peace of mind ;
And the new-year's coming up, mother, but I shall never see
The blossom on the blackthorn, the leaf upon the tree.

Last May we made a crown of flowers: we had a merry day;
Beneath the hawthorn on the green they made me Queen of May;
And we danced about the maypole, and in the hazel copse,
Till Charles's wain came out above the tall white chimney-tops.

There's not a flower on all the hills: the frost is on the pane:
I only wish to live till the snowdrops come again:
I wish the snow would melt and the sun come out on high:
I long to see a flower so before the day I die.

The building rook'll caw from the windy tall elm-tree,
And the tufted plover pipe along the fallow lea,
And the swallow'll come back again with Summer o'er the wave,
But I shall lie alone, mother, within the mouldering grave.

Upon the chancel-casement, and upon that grave of mine,
In the early early morning the Summer sun'll shine,
Before the red cock crows from the farm upon the hill,
When you are warm asleep, mother, and all the world is still.

When the flowers come again, mother, beneath the
   waning light,
You'll never see me more in the long grey fields at
   night;
When from the dry dark wold the Summer airs
   blow cool
On the oat-grass, and the sword-grass, and the
   bulrush in the pool.

You'll bury me, my mother, just beneath the hawthorn shade,
And you'll come sometimes and see me where I am
   lowly laid.
I shall not forget you, mother, I shall hear you when
   you pass,
With your feet above my head in the long and
   pleasant grass.

I have been wild and wayward, but you'll forgive
   me now;
You'll kiss me, my own mother, on my cheek and
   on my brow.
Nay, nay, you must not weep, nor let your grief be
   wild,
You should not fret for me, mother, you have
   another child.

If I can I'll come again, mother, from out my
   resting-place;
Though you'll not see me, mother, I shall look upon
   your face;
Though I cannot speak a word, I shall hearken
   what you say,
And be often, often with you, when you think I'm
   far away.

P

Good-night, good-night, when I have said, Good-
  night for evermore,
And you see me carried out from the threshold of
  the door;
Don't let Effie come to see me, till my grave be
  growing green:
She'll be a better child to you than I have ever
  been.

She'll find my garden-tools upon the granary floor:
Let her take 'em: they are hers: I shall never
  garden more:
But tell her, when I'm gone, to train the rose-bush
  that I set
About the parlour-window, and the box of migno-
  nette.

Good-night, sweet mother: call me before the day
  is born.
All night I lie awake, but I fall asleep at morn;
But I would see the sun rise upon the glad new-
  year,
So, if you're waking, call me, call me early, mother
  dear.

I thought to pass away before, and yet alive I am;
And in the fields all round, I hear the bleating of
  the lamb.
How sadly, I remember, rose the morning of the
  year!
To die before the snowdrop came, and now the
  violet's here.

O sweet is the new violet, that comes beneath the
    skies,
And sweeter is the young lamb's voice to me that
    cannot rise ;
And sweet is all the land about, and all the flowers
    that blow,
And sweeter far is death than life to me that long
    to go.

It seem'd so hard at first, mother, to leave the
    blessèd sun,
And now it seems as hard to stay, and yet His will
    be done !
But still I think it can't be long before I find release;
And that good man, the clergyman, has told me
    words of peace.

O blessings on his kindly voice and on his silver
    hair !
And blessings on his whole life long, until he meet
    me there !
O blessings on his kindly heart and on his silver
    head !
A thousand times I blest him, as he knelt beside
    my bed.

He taught me all the mercy, for he show'd me all
    the sin ;
Now, though my lamp was lighted late, there's One
    will let me in :
Nor would I now be well, mother, again, if that
    could be,
For my desire is but to pass to Him that died for
    me.

I did not hear the dog howl, mother, or the death-
    watch beat,
There came a sweeter token when the night and
    morning meet;
But sit beside my bed, mother, and put your hand
    in mine,
And Effie on the other side, and I will tell the sign.

All in the wild March-morning, I heard the angels
    call;
It was when the moon was setting, and the dark
    was over all;
The trees began to whisper, and the wind began to
    roll,
And in the wild March-morning I heard them call
    my soul.

For lying broad awake I thought of you and Effie
    dear;
I saw you sitting in the house, and I no longer
    here.
With all my strength I pray'd for both, and so I felt
    resign'd,
And up the valley came a swell of music on the
    wind.

I thought that it was fancy, and I listen'd in my
    bed,
And then did something speak to me,—I know not
    what was said;
For great delight and shuddering took hold of all
    my mind,
And up the valley came again the music on the
    wind.

But you were sleeping ; and I said, "It's not for
    them: 'tis mine."
And if it comes three times, I thought, I take it for
    a sign.
And once again it came, and close beside the
    window-bars,
Then seem'd to go right up to Heaven and die
    among the stars.

So now I think my time is near ; I trust it is ; I
    know
The blessèd music went that way my soul will have
    to go.
And for myself, indeed, I care not if I go to-day.
But, Effie, you must comfort her when I am past
    away.

O look ! the sun begins to rise, the heavens are in
    a glow,
He shines upon a hundred fields, and all of them I
    know.
And there I move no longer now, and there his
    light may shine—
Wild flowers in the valley for other hands than
    mine.

O sweet and strange it seems to me, that ere this
    day is done,
The voice, that now is speaking, may be beyond the
    sun—
For ever and for ever with those just souls and
    true—
And what is life that we should moan ? why make
    we such ado ?

For ever and for ever all in a blessèd home,
And there to wait a little while, till you and Effie come—
To lie within the light of God, as I lie upon your breast,
And the wicked cease from troubling, and the weary are at rest.

A. Tennyson

CLXV
LITTLE WILLIE

Poor little Willie,
    With his many pretty wiles;
Worlds of wisdom in his look,
    And quaint, quiet smiles;
Hair of amber, touch'd with
    Gold of Heaven so brave;
All lying darkly hid
    In a workhouse grave.

You remember little Willie,
    Fair and funny fellow! he
Sprang like a lily
    From the dirt of poverty.
Poor little Willie!
    Not a friend was nigh,
When from the cold world
    He crouch'd down to die.

In the day we wander'd foodless,
    Little Willie cried for "bread;"
In the night we wander'd homeless,
    Little Willie cried for "bed."

Parted at the workhouse door,
   Not a word we said ;
Ah ! so tired was poor Willie !
   And so sweetly sleep the dead !

'Twas in the dead of winter
   We laid him in the earth ;
The world brought in the new year
   On a tide of mirth.
But, for lost little Willie
   Not a tear we crave ;
Cold and hunger cannot wake him
   In his workhouse grave.

We thought him beautiful,
   Felt it hard to part ;
We loved him dutiful :
   Down, down, poor heart !
The storms they may beat,
   The winter winds may rave ;
Little Willie feels not
   In his workhouse grave.

No room for little Willie ;
   In the world he had no part ;
On him stared the Gorgon-eye
   Through which looks no heart.
" Come to me," said Heaven ;
   And if Heaven will save,
Little matters though the door
   Be a workhouse grave.
                  Gerald Massey

VI

THE HEART

CLXVI

CHRIST TO THE SINNER

Hark, my soul! it is the Lord,
'Tis thy Saviour, hear His word;
Jesus speaks, and speaks to thee;
"Say, poor sinner, lov'st thou Me?

" I deliver'd thee when bound,
And, when bleeding, heal'd thy wound;
Sought thee wandering, set thee right,
Turn'd thy darkness into light.

" Can a woman's tender care
Cease towards the child she bare?
Yes, she may forgetful be,
Yet will I remember thee!

" Mine is an unchanging love,
Higher than the heights above,
Deeper than the depths beneath,
Free and faithful, strong as death.

"Thou shalt see my glory soon,
When the work of grace is done;
Partner of my throne shalt be;
Say, poor sinner, lov'st thou Me?"

Lord, it is my chief complaint,
That my love is weak and faint;
Yet I love Thee, and adore!
O! for grace to love Thee more.

W. Cowper

CLXVII
SUBMISSION

O Lord! how happy should we be
If we could cast our care on Thee,
   If we from self could rest;
And feel at heart that One above,
In perfect wisdom, perfect love,
   Is working for the best.

How far from this our daily life!
Ever disturb'd by anxious strife,
   By sudden wild alarms;
O could we but relinquish all
Our earthly props, and simply fall
   On Thy almighty arms!

Could we but kneel and cast our load,
E'en while we pray, upon our God,
   Then rise with lightened cheer,
Sure that the Father, who is nigh
To still the famish'd raven's cry,
   Will hear, in that we fear.

We cannot trust Him as we should,
So chafes fall'n nature's restless mood
   To cast its peace away;
Yet birds and flow'rets round us preach,
All, all the present evil teach
   Sufficient for the day.

Lord, make these faithless hearts of ours
Such lessons learn from birds and flowers,
   Make them from self to cease;
Leave all things to a Father's will,
And taste, before Him lying still,
   E'en in affliction peace.
Child's Christian Year

CLXVIII

THE STRANGER

Behold! a Stranger's at the door!
He gently knocks, has knock'd before,
Has waited long, is waiting still;
You treat no other friend so ill.

But will He prove a Friend indeed?
He will! the very Friend you need!
The Man of Nazareth, 'tis He,
With garments dyed at Calvary.

If thou art poor, (and poor thou art,)
Lo! He has riches to impart;
Not wealth, in which mean avarice rolls;
O better far! the wealth of souls!

Thou'rt blind; He'll take the scales away,
And let in everlasting day;
Naked Thou art; but He shall dress
Thy blushing soul in Righteousness.

Art thou a weeper? Grief shall fly;
For who can weep with Jesus by?
No terror shall thy hopes annoy;
No tear except the tear of joy.

Admit Him, for the human breast
Ne'er entertain'd so kind a guest:
Admit Him, for you can't expel;
Where'er He comes, He comes to dwell.

Admit Him, ere His anger burn;
His feet departed, ne'er return!
Admit Him, or the hour's at hand,
When at His door denied you'll stand.

J. Grigg

CLXIX

THE VOICE OF JESUS

I heard the voice of Jesus say,
  "Come unto Me and rest;
Lay down, thou weary one, lay down
  Thy head upon my breast."
I came to Jesus as I was,
  Weary, and worn, and sad,
I found in Him a resting-place,
  And He has made me glad.

I heard the voice of Jesus say,
  "Behold! I freely give
The living water; thirsty one,
  Stoop down, and drink, and live!"
I came to Jesus, and I drank
  Of that life-giving stream;
My thirst was quench'd, my soul revived,
  And now I live in Him.

I heard the voice of Jesus say,
  "I am this dark world's light;
Look unto Me, thy morn shall rise,
  And all thy day be bright."
I look'd to Jesus, and I found
  In Him my star, my sun;
And in that light of life I'll walk
  Till travelling days are done.
                              H. Bonar

CLXX

AFFLICTION

Within this leaf, to every eye
So little worth, doth hidden lie
Most rare and subtle fragrancy.

Wouldst thou its secret strength unbind?
Crush it, and thou shalt perfume find,
Sweet as Arabia's spicy wind.

In this stone, so poor and bare
Of shape and lustre, patient care
Will find for thee a jewel rare.

But first must skilful hands essay
With file and flint to clear away
The film which hides its fire from day.

This leaf? this stone? It is thy heart:
It must be crush'd by pain and smart,
It must be cleans'd by sorrow's art—

Ere it will yield a fragrance sweet,
Ere it will shine, a jewel meet
To lay before thy dear Lord's feet.
                          Bishop Wilberforce

CLXXI

THE HEART'S HOME

Hark! hark! my soul! angelic songs are swelling
O'er earth's green fields and ocean's wave-beat shore,
How sweet the truth those blessed strains are telling,
Of that new life, when sin shall be no more.

Darker than night life's shadows fall around us,
And like benighted men we miss our mark:
God hides Himself, and grace has scarcely found us,
Ere death finds out his victims in the dark.

Onward we go, for still we hear them singing,
"Come weary souls, for Jesus bids you come,"
And thro' the dark, its echoes sweetly ringing,
The music of the gospel leads us home.

Far, far away, like bells at evening pealing,
The voice of Jesus sounds o'er land and sea,
And laden souls by thousands meekly stealing,
Kind Shepherd, turn their weary steps to Thee.

Rest comes at last, though life be long and dreary,
The day must dawn, and darksome night be past,
All journeys end in welcomes to the weary,
And heaven, the heart's true home, will come at last.
F. W. Faber

CLXXII

THE HEART'S LONGING

O Paradise ! O Paradise !
  Who doth not crave for rest ?
Who would not seek the happy land,
  Where they that loved are blest ?
    Where loyal hearts and true
      Stand ever in the light,
    All rapture through and through,
      In God's most holy sight.

O Paradise ! O Paradise !
  'Tis weary waiting here :
We long to be where Jesus is,
  To feel, to see Him near ;
    Where loyal hearts and true
      Stand ever in the light,
    All rapture through and through,
      In God's most holy sight.

O Paradise ! O Paradise !
  We want to sin no more ;
We want to be as pure on earth
  As on thy spotless shore ;
    Where loyal hearts and true
    Stand ever in the light,
    All rapture through and through,
    In God's most holy sight.
                    F. W. Faber

CLXXIII

A PRAYER

Thou, who dost dwell alone—
Thou, who dost know thine own—
Thou, to whom all are known
From the cradle to the grave—
  Save, O save.
From the world's temptations,
From tribulations ;
From that fierce anguish
Wherein we languish ;
From that torpor deep
Wherein we lie asleep,
Heavy as death, cold as the grave ;
  Save, O save.
When the soul, growing clearer,
Sees God no nearer :
When the soul, mounting higher,
To God comes no nigher :
But the arch-fiend, Pride,
Mounts at her side,

Foiling her high emprise,
Sealing her eagle eyes,
And when she fain would soar,
Makes idols to adore;
Changing the pure emotion
Of her high devotion
To a skin-deep sense
Of her own eloquence:
Strong to deceive, strong to enslave—
    Save, O save.
From the ingrain'd fashion
Of this earthly nature
That mars thy creature;
From grief that is but passion;
From mirth that is but feigning;
From tears that bring no healing;
From wild and weak complaining;
  Thine old strength revealing,
    Save, O save.
From doubt where all is double:
Where wise men are not strong:
Where comfort turns to trouble:
Where just men suffer wrong—
Where sorrow treads on joy:
Where sweet things soonest cloy:
Where faiths are built on dust:
Where Love is half mistrust;
Hungry, and barren, and sharp as the sea;
    O, set us free.
O, let the false dream fly
Where our sick souls do lie
Tossing continually.
O, where thy voice doth come

Let all doubts be dumb :
Let all words be mild :
All strife's be reconciled :
All pains beguiled.
Light bring no blindness ;
Love no unkindness ;
Knowledge no ruin ;
Fear no undoing.
From the cradle to the grave,
    Save, O save.
                 Matthew Arnold

CLXXIV

CHRISTIAN COURAGE

O, shame upon thee, listless heart,
  So sad a sigh to heave ;
As if thy Saviour had no part
  In thoughts that make thee grieve.

As if along His lonesome way
  He had not borne for thee
Sad languors through the summer day,
  Storms on the wintry sea.

Thou shalt have joy in sadness soon ;
  The pure, calm hope be thine,
Which brightens, like the eastern morn,
  As day's wild lights decline.
                 J. Keble

CLXXV
LITTLE SINS

Look westward, pensive little one,
How the bright hues together run,
Around where late the waning sun
   Sank in his evening cloud.
Or eastward turn thee, and admire
How linger yet the showers of fire,
Deep in each fold, high on each spire
   Of yonder mountain proud.

Thou seest it not : an envious screen,
A fluttering leaflet, floats between
Thee and that fair mysterious scene,
   A veil too near thine eye.
One finger's breadth at hand will mar
A world of light in Heaven afar,
A mote eclipse a glorious star,
   An eyelid hide the sky.
J. Keble

CLXXVI
LOVE

They sin who tell us love can die.
With life all other passions fly,
   All others are but vanity.
In Heaven ambition cannot dwell,
Nor avarice in the vaults of hell ;
   Earthly, these passions are of earth,
They perish where they have their birth ;
   But love is indestructible

Its holy flame for ever burneth,
From Heaven it came, to Heaven returneth;
Too oft on earth a troubled guest,
At times deceived, at times opprest,
  It here is tried and purified,
Then hath in Heaven its perfect rest;
It soweth here with toil, and care,
But the harvest-time of Love is there.
O, when a mother meets on high,
  The babe she lost in infancy,
Hath she not then for pains, and fears,
  The days of woe, the watchful night,
For all her sorrow, all her tears,
  An over-payment of delight.
R. Southey

CLXXVII

CALM

Calm me, my God, and keep me calm,
  Whilst these hot breezes blow;
Be like the night-dew's cooling balm
  Upon earth's fever'd brow!

Calm me, my God, and keep me calm,
  Soft resting on Thy breast;
Soothe me with holy hymn and psalm,
  And bid my spirit rest.

Calm me, my God, and keep me calm,
  Let Thine outstretchèd wing
Be like the shade of Elim's palm
  Beside her desert-spring.

Yes ; keep me calm, though loud and rude
   The sounds my ear that greet ;
Calm in the closet's solitude,
   Calm in the bustling street ;

Calm in the hour of buoyant health,
   Calm in my hour of pain ;
Calm in my poverty or wealth,
   Calm in my loss or gain ;

Calm in the sufferance of wrong,
   Like Him who bore my shame ;
Calm mid the threat'ning, taunting throng,
   Who hate Thy holy Name.

Calm as the ray of sun or star,
   Which storms assail in vain,
Moving unruffled through earth's war
   Th' eternal calm to gain !

H. Bonar

CLXXVIII

RETIREMENT

Far from the world, O Lord, I flee,
   From strife and tumult far ;
From scenes where Satan wages still
   His most successful war.

The calm retreat, the silent shade,
   With prayer and praise agree,
And seem by Thy sweet bounty made
   For those who follow Thee.

There, if Thy spirit touch the soul,
  And grace her mean abode,
O, with what peace, and joy, and love,
  She communes with her God!

There, like the nightingale, she pours
  Her solitary lays,
Nor asks a witness of her song,
  Nor thirsts for human praise.

Author and Guardian of my life;
  Sweet Source of light Divine;
And, all harmonious names in one,
  My Saviour! Thou art mine!

What thanks I owe Thee, and what love,
  A boundless, endless store,
Shall echo through the realms above,
  When time shall be no more.
                W. Cowper

CLXXIX

THE HEART'S SONG

In the silent midnight watches,
  List—thy bosom door!
How it knocketh, knocketh, knocketh,
  Knocketh evermore!
Say not 'tis thy pulse's beating;
  'Tis thy heart of sin:
'Tis thy Saviour knocks, and crieth,
  Rise, and let Me in!

Death comes down with reckless footstep
  To the hall and hut:
Think you Death will stand a-knocking
  Where the door is shut?
Jesus waiteth— waiteth—waiteth;
  But thy door is fast!
Grieved, away thy Saviour goeth:
  Death breaks in at last.

Then 'tis thine to stand entreating
  Christ to let thee in:
At the gate of heaven beating,
  Wailing for thy sin.
Nay, alas! thou foolish virgin,
  Hast thou then forgot,
Jesus waited long to know thee,
  But He knows thee not!
A. C. Coxe

CLXXX

REALITY

Love thy God, and love Him only,
And thy breast shall ne'er be lonely;
In that one great Spirit meet
All things mighty, grave, and sweet.
Vainly strives the soul to mingle
With a being of our kind:
Vainly hearts with hearts are twined;
For the deepest still is single.
An impalpable resistance
Holds like natures at a distance.
Mortal! love that Holy One,
Or for ever dwell alone.
A. De Vere

CLXXXI
LONGING FOR CHRIST

My spirit longs for Thee
  Within my troubled breast,
Although I be unworthy
  Of so Divine a Guest.

Of so Divine a Guest
  Unworthy though I be,
Yet has my heart no rest
  Unless it come from Thee.

Unless it come from Thee,
  In vain I look around ;
In all that I can see
  No rest is to be found.

No rest is to be found,
  But in Thy blessèd love.
O let my wish be crown'd,
  And send it from above !

J. Byrom

CLXXXII
LONGING TO BE WITH CHRIST

Let me be with Thee where Thou art,
  My Saviour, my eternal Rest !
Then only will this longing heart
  Be fully and for ever blest !

Let me be with Thee where Thou art,
  Thy unveil'd glory to behold;
Then only will this wandering heart
  Cease to be treacherous, faithless, cold!

Let me be with Thee where Thou art,
  Where spotless saints Thy Name adore;
Then only will this sinful heart
  Be evil and defiled no more!

Let me be with Thee where Thou art,
  Where none can die, and none remove,
Where neither death nor life will part
  Me from Thy Presence and Thy love!
C. Elliott

CLXXXIII

THE HAPPY SOUL

O happy soul, that lives on high,
  While men lie grovelling here!
His hopes are fix'd above the sky,
  And faith forbids his fear.

His conscience knows no secret stings;
  While peace and joy combine
To form a life, whose holy springs
  Are hidden and divine.

He waits in secret on his God,
  His God in secret sees;
Let earth be all in arms abroad,
  He dwells in heavenly peace.

His pleasures rise from things unseen,
  Beyond this world and time,
Where neither eyes nor ears have been,
  Nor thoughts of sinners climb.

He wants no pomp, nor royal throne,
  To raise his figure here :
Content and pleased to live unknown,
  Till Christ, his Life, appear.

He looks to Heaven's eternal hill,
  To meet that glorious day ;
And patient waits his Saviour's will,
  To fetch his soul away.
                              I. Watts

CLXXXIV

RESIGNATION

Is Resignation's lesson hard ?
  Examine, we shall find
That duty gives up little more
  Than anguish of the mind.

Grief's most inglorious coward tears
  From brutal eyes have ran ;
Smiles, incommunicable smiles,
  Are radiant marks of man.

They cast a sudden glory round
  The illumined human face ;
And light in sons of honest joy
  Some beams of Moses' face.

Resign, and all the load of life
  That moment you remove;
Its heavy tax, ten thousand cares
  Devolve on One above;

Who bids us lay our burden down
  On His Almighty hand;
Softens our duty to relief,
  To blessing, His command.

For joy what cause? how every sense
  Is courted from above!
The year around with presents rich,
  The growth of endless love!

But most o'erlook the blessings pour'd,
  Forget the wonders done,
And terminate, wrapt up in sense,
  Their prospect at the sun.

From that, their final point of view,
  From that, their radiant goal,
On travel infinite of thought
  Sets out the nobler soul—

Broke loose from time's tenacious ties
  And earth's involving gloom,
To range at last its vast domain,
  And talk with worlds to come.

Who would not with an heart at ease,
  Bright eye, unclouded brow,
Wisdom and goodness at the helm,
  The roughest ocean plough?

Thy will is welcome, let it wear
  Its most tremendous form ;
Roar waves! rage winds! I know that Thou
  Canst save me by a storm.

For what is Resignation ? 'tis
  Man's weakness understood ;
And wisdom grasping with an hand
  Far stronger, every good.

E. Young

CLXXXV
CONSCIENCE

My conscience is my crown :
  Contented thoughts my rest ;
My heart is happy in itself ;
  My bliss is in my breast.

Enough, I reckon wealth ;
  A mean, the surest lot ;
That lies too high for base contempt,
  Too low for envy's shot.

My wishes are but few,
  All easy to fulfil :
I make the limits of my power
  The bounds unto my will.

I feel no care of coin ;
  Well-doing is my wealth :
My mind to me an empire is
  While Grace affordeth health.

I wrestle not with rage,
  While fury's flame doth burn;
It is in vain to stop the stream,
  Until the tide doth turn.

But when the flame is out,
  And ebbing wrath doth end;
I turn a late enragèd foe
  Into a quiet friend;

And taught with often proof,
  A temper'd calm I find
To be most solace to itself,
  Best cure for angry mind.

No change of fortune's calms
  Can cast my comforts down;
When fortune smiles, I smile to think
  How quickly she will frown;

And when, in froward mood,
  She moved an angry foe,
Small gain I found to let her come,
  Less loss to let her go.
                              R. Southwell

CLXXXVI

RETURN

Return, O wanderer, to thy home;
  Thy Father calls for thee:
No longer now an exile roam,
  In guilt and misery,
    Return, return!

Return, O wanderer, to thy home;
'Tis Jesus calls for thee:
The Spirit and the Bride say, Come:
O now for refuge flee;
Return, return!

Return, O wanderer, to thy home;
'Tis madness to delay;
There are no pardons in the tomb,
And brief is mercy's day:
Return, return!

Thos. Hastings

CLXXXVII
JUST AS I AM

Just as I am, without one plea
But that Thy Blood was shed for me,
And that Thou bidd'st me come to Thee,
O Lamb of God, I come.

Just as I am, and waiting not
To rid my soul of one dark blot,
To Thee, whose Blood can cleanse each spot,
O Lamb of God, I come!

Just as I am, though toss'd about
With many a conflict, many a doubt,
Fightings and fears within, without,
O Lamb of God, I come!

Just as I am, poor, wretched, blind.
Sight, riches, healing of the mind,
Yea, all I need, in Thee to find,
O Lamb of God, I come!

Just as I am, Thou wilt receive,
Wilt welcome, pardon, cleanse, relieve !
Because Thy promise I believe,
    O Lamb of God, I come !

Just as I am, (Thy Love unknown
Has broken every barrier down,)
Now, to be Thine, yea, Thine alone,
    O Lamb of God, I come

Just as I am, of that free love
The breadth, length, depth, and height to prove,
Here for a season, then above,
    O Lamb of God, I come !
C. Elliott

CLXXXVIII

ABIDE WITH ME

Abide with me ! fast falls the even-tide ;
The darkness deepens ; Lord, with me abide !
When other helpers fail, and comforts flee,
Help of the helpless, O abide with me.

Swift to its close ebbs out life's little day ;
Earth's joys grow dim, its glories pass away ;
Change and decay in all around I see ;
O Thou, who changest not, abide with me !

Not a brief glance I beg, a passing word ;
But, as Thou dwell'st with Thy disciples, Lord,
Familiar, condescending, patient, free,
Come, not to sojourn, but abide, with me.

Come not in terrors, as the King of kings;
But kind and good, with healing in Thy wings;
Tears for all woes, a heart for every plea;
Come, Friend of sinners, and thus bide with me.

I need Thy Presence every passing hour,
What but Thy grace can foil the Tempter's power?
Who like Thyself my guide and stay can be?
Through cloud and sunshine, O abide with me!

Hold Thou Thy cross before my closing eyes;
Shine through the gloom, and point me to the skies!
Heaven's morning breaks, and earth's vain shadows
    flee;
In life, in death, O Lord, abide with me!

H. F. Lyte

CLXXXIX

REST

Of all the thoughts of God that are
Borne inward unto souls afar,
   Along the Psalmist's music deep—
Now tell me if that any is,
For gift or grace, surpassing this—
   " He giveth His belovèd sleep?"

What would we give to our beloved?
The hero's heart to be unmoved—
   The poet's star-tuned harp to sweep—
The senate's shout for patriot vows—
The monarch's crown to light the brows?
   " He giveth His belovèd sleep."

What do we give to our beloved?
A little faith not all unproved—
   A little dust to overweep—
And bitter memories to make
The whole earth blasted for our sake?
   " He giveth His belovèd sleep."

Sleep, soft beloved! we sometimes say,
But have no power to chase away
   Sad dreams that through the eyelids creep;
But never doleful dream again
Shall break the happy slumber, when
   He giveth His belovèd sleep."

O earth, so full of dreary noises!
O men, with wailing in your voices!
   O delvèd gold, the wailer's heap!
O strife, O curse that o'er it fall!
God makes a silence through you all,
   And " giveth His belovèd sleep."

His dews drop mutely on the hill;
His cloud above it saileth still,
   Though on its slope men toil and reap!
More softly than the dew is shed,
Or cloud is floated overhead,
   " He giveth His belovèd sleep."

Yea! men may wonder, while they scan
A living, thinking, feeling man,
   Sufficient such a rest to keep;
But angels say,—and through the word
The motion of their smile is heard—
   " He giveth His belovèd sleep."

For me, my heart that erst did go
Most like a tired child at a show,
  Seeing through tears the juggler leap—
Would fain its weary vision close
And childlike on His love repose,
  Who "giveth His belovèd sleep."

And Friends—dear Friends—when it shall be
That this low breath is gone from me,—
  When round my bier ye come to weep;
Let one most loving of you all
Say, "Not a tear for her must fall,
  He giveth His belovèd sleep."
            E. B. Browning

CXC
"*SOON—AND FOR EVER*"
Soon and for ever!
  Such promise our trust,
Though ashes to ashes
  And dust unto dust;
Soon—and for ever
  Our union shall be
Made perfect, our glorious
  Redeemer, in Thee.
When the sins and the sorrows
  Of time shall be o'er;
Its pangs and its partings
  Remember'd no more;
When life cannot fail,
  And when death cannot sever,
Christians with Christ shall be
  Soon—and for ever.

R

Soon—and for ever
  The breaking of day
Shall drive all the dark clouds
  Of sorrow away.
Soon—and for ever
  We'll see as we're seen,
And learn the deep meaning
  Of things that have been.
When fightings without us,
  And fears from within,
Shall weary no more
  In the warfare of sin.
Where tears, and where fears,
  And where death shall be—never,
Christians with Christ shall be
  Soon—and for ever.

Soon—and for ever
  The work shall be done,
The warfare accomplished,
  The victory won.
Soon—and for ever
  The soldier lay down
His sword for a harp,
  And his cross for a crown.
Then droop not in sorrow,
  Despond not in fear,
A glorious to-morrow
  Is brightening and near;
When—blessed reward
  Of each faithful endeavour,
Christians with Christ shall be
  Soon—and for ever.
                    J. S. Monsell

CXCI
PEACE
My soul, there is a country
  Afar beyond the stars,
Where stands a winged sentry
  All skilful in the wars.
There, above noise and danger,
  Sweet Peace sits crown'd with smiles,
And One born in a manger
  Commands the beauteous files.
He is thy gracious friend,
  And (O my soul, awake!)
Did in pure love descend
  To die here for thy sake.
If thou canst get but thither,
  There grows the flower of peace,
The Rose that cannot wither,
  Thy fortress, and thy ease.
Leave then thy foolish ranges;
  For none can thee secure,
But One who never changes,
  Thy God, thy life, thy cure.
H. Vaughan

CXCII
THY WILL BE DONE
My God, my Father, while I stray
Far from my home in life's rough way,
O, teach me from my heart to say—
    "Thy will be done!

The Sunday

Though dark my path, and sad my lot,
Let me be still and murmur not;
And breathe the prayer divinely taught—
   "Thy will be done!"

What though in lonely grief I sigh
For friends belov'd no longer nigh,
Submissive still would I reply—
   "Thy will be done!"

If thou shouldst call me to resign
What most I prize—it ne'er was mine;
I only yield Thee what was Thine:
   "Thy will be done!"

Should pining sickness waste away
My life in premature decay,
My Father—still I'll strive to say,
   "Thy will be done!"

If but my fainting heart be blest
With Thy Spirit for its guest,
My God, to Thee I leave the rest,
   "Thy will be done!"

Renew my will from day to day,
Blend it with Thine, and take away
All that now makes it hard to say,
   "Thy will be done!"

Then, when on earth I breathe no more
The prayer oft mix'd with tears before,
I'll sing upon a happier shore,
   "Thy will be done!"

C. Elliott

CXCIII

CONFIDENCE

Through the love of God, our Saviour,
    All will be well;
Free and changeless is His favour;
    All, all is well!
Precious is the Blood that heal'd us,
Perfect is the grace that seal'd us,
Strong the hand stretch'd out to shield us;
    All must be well!

Though we pass through tribulation,
    All will be well;
Ours is such a full salvation—
    All, all is well!
Happy, still in God confiding,
Fruitful, if in Christ abiding,
Holy, through the Spirit's guiding;
    All must be well!

We expect a bright to-morrow,
    All will be well;
Faith can sing through days of sorrow,
    All, all is well!
On our Father's love relying,
Jesus every need supplying,
Or in living, or in dying.
    All must be well!

Anon.

CXCIV
THE CONQUEST OF PRIDE

I look'd with pride on what I'd done,
I counted merits o'er anew,
In presence of the burning sun,
Which drinks me like a drop of dew.
A lofty scorn I dared to shed
On human passions, hopes and jars,
I—standing on the countless dead,
And pitied by the countless stars.

But mine is now a humbled heart,
My lonely pride is weak as tears ;
No more I seek to stand apart,
A mocker of the rolling years.
Imprison'd in this wintry clime,
I've found enough, O Lord, of breath,
Enough to plume the feet of time,
Enough to hide the eyes of death.

A. Smith

CXCV
PRIDE OF REASON

In pride, in reasoning pride our error lies ;
All quit their sphere, and rush into the skies.
Pride still is aiming at the blest abodes,
Men would be angels, angels would be Gods.
Aspiring to be Gods, if angels fell,
Aspiring to be angels, men rebel ;
And who but wishes to invert the laws
Of order, sins against th' Eternal cause.

A. Pope

CXCVI
THE CALL

Child of sin and sorrow,
  Fill'd with dismay,
Wait not for to-morrow,
  Yield thee to-day!
    Heaven bids thee come
    While yet there's room:
Child of sin and sorrow,
  Hear, and obey!

Child of sin and sorrow,
  Why wilt thou die?
Come, while thou canst borrow
  Help from on high!
    Grieve not that love
    Which from above,
Child of sin and sorrow,
  Would bring thee nigh.
T. Hastings

CXCVII
PRAYER AT MIDNIGHT

The stars shine bright while earth is dark!
  While all the woods are dumb,
How clear those far-off silver chimes
  From tower and turret come.

Chilly but sweet, the midnight air:
  And lo! with every sound,
Down from the ivy-leaf a drop
  Falls glittering on the ground.

The Sunday

'Twas night when Christ was born on earth;
   Night heard his first, faint cry;
While angels caroll'd round the star
   Of the Epiphany.

Alas! and is our love too weak
   To meet Him on His way?
To pray for nations in their sleep?
   For Love then let us pray.

Pray for the millions slumbering now;
   The sick who cannot sleep;
O may those sweet sounds waft them thoughts
   As peaceful, and as deep.

Pray for th' unholy, and the vain:
   O, may that pure-toned bell
Disperse the demon powers of air,
   And evil dreams dispel!

And ever let us wing our prayer
   With praise: and ever say,
Glory to God who makes the night
   Benignant as the day!

A. D. Vere

CXCVIII
THE UNBELIEVER

Behold yon wretch, by impious passion driven,
Believes and trembles while he scoffs at Heaven ;
By weakness strong, and bold thro' fear alone,
He dreads the sneer by shallow coxcombs thrown ;
Dauntless pursues the path Spinoza trod ;
To man a coward, and a brave to God.

A. Pope

CXCIX
SEEDS OF LIGHT

God scatters love on every side,
  Freely among his children all,
And always hearts are lying open wide
  Wherein some grains may fall.

There is no wind but soweth seeds
  Of a more true and open life,
Which burst, unlook d for, into high-soul'd deeds,
  With wayside beauty rife.

We find within these souls of ours
  Some wild germs of a higher birth,
Which in the poet's tropic heart bear flowers
  Whose fragrance fills the earth.

Within the hearts of all men lie
  Those promises of wider bliss,
Which blossom into hopes that cannot die,
  In sunny hours like this.

J. R. Lowell

CC

ST. AGNES' EVE

Deep on the convent-roof the snows
    Are sparkling to the moon :
My breath to Heaven like vapour goes,
    May my soul follow soon !
The shadows of the convent towers
    Slant down the snowy sward,
Still creeping with the creeping hours
    That lead me to my Lord :
Make thou my spirit pure and clear
    As are the frosty skies,
Or this first snowdrop of the year
    That in my bosom lies.

As these white robes are soil'd, and dark,
    To yonder shining ground ;
As this pale taper's earthly spark,
    To yonder argent round ;
So shows my soul before the Lamb,
    My spirit before Thee,
So in mine earthly house I am
    To that I hope to be.
Break up the heavens, O Lord ! and far,
    Thro' all yon starlight keen,
Draw me, Thy bride, a glittering star
    In raiment white, and clean.

He lifts me to the golden doors,
   The flashes come, and go ;
All heaven bursts her starry floors,
   And strows her lights below,
And deepens on and up, the gates
   Roll back, and far within
For me the Heavenly Bridegroom waits,
   To make me pure of sin.
The sabbaths of eternity,
   One Sabbath deep and wide—
A light upon the shining sea,
   The Bridegroom, and His bride.
A. Tennyson

VII

NATURE

CCI

PSALM XIX

The spacious firmament on high,
With all the blue ethereal sky,
And spangled Heavens, a shining frame,
Their great Original proclaim.
The unwearied sun, from day to day,
Does his Creator's power display,
And publishes to every land
The work of an Almighty hand.

Soon as the evening shades prevail
The moon takes up the wondrous tale,
And nightly to the listening earth
Repeats the story of her birth;
Whilst all the stars that round her burn,
And all the planets in their turn,
Confirm the tidings as they roll,
And spread the truth from pole to pole.

What, though in solemn silence all
Move round the dark terrestrial ball;
What, though no real voice or sound
Amidst their radiant orbs be found,

In reason's ear they all rejoice,
And utter forth a glorious voice,
For ever singing as they shine,
" The hand that made us is Divine."
     Joseph Addison

CCII

NATURE

Beautiful are the heralds
 That stand at Nature's door,
Crying, " O traveller, enter in,
 And taste the Master's store !"
One or the other always crying—
 In the voice of the summer hours,
In the thunder of the winter storm,
 Or the song of the fresh spring flowers.

" Enter," they cry, "to a kingly feast,
 Where all may venture near ;
A million beauties for the eye,
 And music for the ear:
Only, before thou enterest in,
 Upon the threshold fall,
And pay the tribute of thy praise
 ' To Him who gives thee all.' "

So some kneel down and enter
 With reverent step and slow ;
And calm airs fraught with precious scent
 Breathe round them as they go :
Gently they pass 'mid sight and sound
 And the sunshine round them sleeping,
To where the angels, Faith and Love,
 The inner gates are keeping.

    Then backward rolls the wondrous screen
        That hides the secret place,
    Where the God of Nature veils Himself
        In the brighter realms of grace :—
    But they who have not bent the knee
        Will smile at this my story :
    For, though they enter the temple gates,
        They know not the inner glory.
                        W. E. Littlewood

CCIII

THE GLORY OF GOD IN CREATION

    Thou art, O God! the life and light
        Of all this wondrous world we see ;
    Its glow by day, its smile by night,
        Are but reflections caught from Thee.
Where'er we turn thy glories shine,
And all things fair and bright are thine.

    When day, with farewell beam, delays
        Among the opening clouds of even,
    And we can almost think we gaze
        Through golden vistas into Heaven—
Those hues, that make the sun's decline
So soft, so radiant, Lord! are thine.

    When night, with wings of starry gloom,
        O'ershadows all the earth and skies,
    Like some dark, beauteous bird, whose plume
        Is sparkling with unnumber'd eyes—
That sacred gloom, those fires divine,
So grand, so countless, Lord! are thine.

When youthful spring around us breathes,
Thy Spirit warms her fragrant sigh ;
And every flower the summer wreathes
Is born beneath that kindling eye.
Where'er we turn Thy glories shine,
And all things fair, and bright, are Thine.
T. Moore

CCIV

NATURE AND HEAVEN

I praised the earth, in beauty seen
With garlands gay of various green ;
I praised the sea, whose ample field
Shone glorious as a silver shield ;
And earth and ocean seem'd to say,
" Our beauties are but for a day."

I praised the sun, whose chariot roll'd
On wheels of amber, and of gold ;
I praised the moon, whose softer eye
Gleam'd sweetly through the summer sky ;
And moon, and sun, in answer said,
" Our days of light are numberèd."

O God ! O good beyond compare !
If thus Thy meaner works are fair,
If thus Thy bounties gild the span
Of ruin'd earth, and sinful man,
How glorious must the mansion be,
Where Thy redeem'd shall dwell with Thee !
Bishop Heber

CCV
THE BETTER LAND

I hear thee speak of the better land;
Thou call'st its children a happy band;
Mother! O, where is that radiant shore,—
Shall we not seek it and weep no more?
Is it where the flower of the orange blows,
And the fire-flies dance through the myrtle boughs?
       "Not there, not there, my child!"

Is it where the feathery palm trees rise,
And the date grows ripe under sunny skies,
Or 'midst the green islands of glittering seas
Where fragrant forests perfume the breeze,
And strange, bright birds on their starry wings
Bear the rich hues of all glorious things?
       "Not there, not there, my child!"

Is it far away in some region old
Where the rivers wander o'er sands of gold—
Where the burning rays of the ruby shine,
And the diamond lights up the secret mine,
And the pearl gleams forth from the coral strand—
Is it there, sweet mother, that better land?
       "Not there, not there, my child!"

Eye hath not seen it, my gentle boy!
Ear hath not heard its deep songs of joy,
Dreams cannot picture a world so fair,
Sorrow and death may not enter there;
Time doth not breathe on its faultless bloom,
For beyond the clouds, and beyond the tomb,
       It is there, it is there, my child!
               Mrs. Hemans

CCVI

A CHILD'S FIRST IMPRESSION OF A STAR

She had been told that God made all the stars
That twinkled up in heaven, and now she stood
Watching the coming of the twilight on,
As if it were a new and perfect world,
And this was its first eve. She stood alone
By the lone window, with the silken lash
Of her soft eye upraised, and her sweet mouth
Half-parted with the new and strange delight
Of beauty that she could not comprehend,
And had not seen before. The purple folds
Of the low sunset clouds, and the blue sky
That look'd so still and delicate above,
Fill'd her young heart with gladness; and the eve
Stole on with its deep shadows, and she still
Stood looking at the west with that half-smile,
As if a pleasant dream were at her heart.
Presently, in the edge of the last tint
Of sunset, where the blue was melted in
To the faint golden mellowness, a star
Stood suddenly. A laugh of wild delight
Burst from her lips, and putting up her hands,
Her simple thought broke forth expressively—
" Father! dear father! God has made a star!"

N. P. Willis

CCVII

HYMN TO THE SEASONS

When Spring unlocks the flowers to paint the laughing soil,
When Summer's balmy showers refresh the mower's toil,
When Winter binds in frosty chains the fallow and the flood,
In God the earth rejoiceth still, and owns its Maker good.

The birds that wake the morning, and those that love the shade ;
The winds that sweep the mountain, or lull the drowsy glade ;
The sun that from his amber bower rejoiceth on his way ;
The moon, and stars, their Maker's name in silent pomp display.

Shall man, the lord of nature, expectant of the sky,—
Shall man, alone unthankful, his little praise deny ?
No ; let the year forsake his course, the seasons cease to be,
Thee, Master, must we always love, and, Saviour, honour Thee.

The flowers of Spring may wither,—the hope of
    Summer fade,—
The Autumn droop in Winter,—the birds forsake
    the shade,—
The wind be lull'd,—the sun and moon forget their
    old decree,
But we in Nature's latest hour, O Lord! will cling
    to Thee.

Bishop Heber

CCVIII

THE LONGEST DAY.

Let us quit the leafy arbour,
   And the torrent murmuring by;
For the sun is in his harbour,
   Weary of the open sky.

Evening now unbinds the fetters
   Fashion'd by the glowing light;
All that breathe are thankful debtors
   To the harbinger of night.

Yet by some grave thoughts attended
   Eve renews her calm career;
For the day that now is ended,
   Is the longest of the year.

Summer ebbs; each day that follows
   Is a reflux from on high,
Tending to the darksome hollows
   Where the frosts of winter lie.

He who governs the creation,
  In His providence, assigned
Such a gradual declination
  To the life of human kind.

Yet we mark it not ; fruits redden,
  Fresh flowers blow, as flowers have blown,
And the heart is loth to deaden
  Hopes that she so long hath known.

Be thou wiser, youthful maiden !
  And, when thy decline shall come,
Let not flowers, or bough fruit-laden,
  Hide the knowledge of thy doom.

Now, e'en now, ere wrapp'd in slumber,
  Fix thine eyes upon the sea
That absorbs time, space, and number,—
  Look thou to eternity !
W. Wordsworth

CCIX

BUBBLES UNDER ICE

Hast thou seen with flash incessant
  Bubbles gliding under ice,
Bodied forth, and evanescent,
  No one knows by what device?

Such are thoughts—a wind-swept meadow
  Mimicking a troubled sea,
Such is life ; and death a shadow
  From the rock Eternity !
W. Wordsworth

CCX

A-MAYING

Yes, surely there's a love abroad
  Through every nerve of Nature playing;
And all between the sky and sod,
  All, all the world has gone a-Maying.

O, wherefore do I sit and give
  My fancy up to idle playing?
Too well I know the half who live,
  One half the world, is not a-Maying.

Where are the dwellers of the lanes,
  The alleys of the stifled city?
Where the waste forms whose sad remains
  Woo death to come for very pity?

Where they who tend the busy loom,
  With pallid cheek, and torn apparel?
The buds they weave will never bloom,
  Their staring birds will never carol.

And where the young of every size
  The factories draw from every bye-way;
Whose violets are each other's eyes,
  But dull as by a dusty highway?

Whose cotton lilies only grow
  'Mid whirring wheels, or jarring spindles?
Their roses in the hectic glow
  To tell how fast the small life dwindles.

Where are the dusky miners?—they
　Who, ever in the earth descending,
Know well the night before their May
　Is one which has in life no ending?

To them 'tis still a joy, I ween,
　To know, while through the darkness going,
That o'er their heads the smiling queen
　Stands with her countless garlands glowing.

O ye who toil in living tombs
　Of light, or dark, no rest receiving,
Far o'er your heads a May time blooms—
　O then be patient, and believing.

Be patient; when earth's winter fails—
　The weary night, which keeps ye staying,—
Then through the broad celestial vales
　Your spirits shall go out a-Maying.
　　　　　　　　　T. B. Read

CCXI

SUNNY DAYS IN WINTER

　Summer is a glorious season,
　　Warm, and bright, and pleasant;
　But the past is not a reason
　　To despise the present:
　So, while health can climb the mountain,
　　And the log lights up the hall,
There are sunny days in winter, after all!

Spring, no doubt, hath faded from us,
  Maiden-like in charms;
Summer, too, with all her promise,
  Perish'd in our arms:
But the memory of the vanish'd
  Whom our hearts recall,
Maketh sunny days in winter, after all!

True, there's scarce a flower that bloometh—
  All the best are dead;
But the wall-flower still perfumeth
  Yonder garden bed;
And the arbutus, pearl-blossom'd,
  Hangs its coral ball:
There are sunny days in winter, after all!

Summer trees are pretty—very,
  And I love them well;
But this holly's glistening berry
  None of those excel.
While the fir can warm the landscape,
  And the ivy clothes the wall,
There are sunny days in winter, after all!

Sunny hours in every season
  Wait the innocent;—
Those who taste with love and reason
  What their God has sent;
Those who neither soar too highly,
  Nor too lowly fall,
Feel the sunny days of winter, after all!

Then, although our darling treasures
    Vanish from the heart ;
Then, although our once-loved pleasures
    One by one depart ;
Though the tomb looms in the distance,
    And the mourning pall,
There is sunshine, and no winter, after all !
                  D. F. Macarthy

CCXII

DUTY

As the hardy oat is growing,
    Howsoe'er the wind may blow ;
As the untired stream is flowing,
    Whether shines the sun or no :—
Thus, though storm-winds rage about it,
    Should the strong plant, Duty, grow—
Thus, with beauty, or without it,
    Should the stream of being flow.
                  D. F. Macarthy

CCXIII

LINES

The lights o'er yonder snowy range,
    Shine yet intense, and tender ;
Or, slowly passing, only change
    From splendour on to splendour.

Before the dying eyes of day
    Immortal visions wander ;
Dreams prescient of a purer ray,
    And morn spread still beyond her.

Lo! heavenward now those gleams expire,
  In heavenly melancholy,
The barrier-mountain, peak, and spire,
  Relinquishing them slowly.

Thus shine, O God! our mortal powers,
  While grief and joy refine them—
And when in death they fade, be ours
  Thus gently to resign them!

A. De Vere

CCXIV

SPRING

Once more, through God's high will and grace,
  Of hours that each its task fulfils,
Heart-healing Spring resumes its place
  The valley through, and scales the hills.

Who knows not Spring? who doubts when blows
  Her breath, that Spring is come indeed?
The swallow doubts not; nor the rose
  That stirs, but wakes not; nor the weed.

Once more the cuckoo's call I hear;
  I know, in many a glen profound,
The earliest violets of the year
  Rise up like water from the ground.

The thorn, I know, once more is white;
  And far down many a forest dale,
The anemones in dubious light
  Are trembling like a bridal veil.

By streams released that surging flow
    From craggy shelf, through sylvan glades,
The pale narcissus, well I know,
    Smiles hour by hour on greener shades.

The honey'd cowslip tufts one more
    The golden slopes ;—with gradual ray
The primrose stars the rock, and o'er
    The wood-path strews its milky way.

I see her not—I feel her near,
    As charioted in mildest airs
She sails through yon empyreal sphere,
    And in her arms and bosom bears

That urn of flowers, and lustral dews,
    Whose sacred balm, on all things shed,
Revives the weak, the old renews,
    And crowns with votive wreaths the dead.
A. De Vere

CCXV

THANKS FOR A SUMMER'S DAY

    The time so tranquil is, and clear,
        That nowhere shall ye find,
    Save on a high and barren hill,
        The air of passing wind.

    All trees and simples, great and small,
        That balmy leaf do bear,
    Than they were painted on a wall,
        No more they move, or stir.

The ample heaven of fabric sure,
  In clearness doth surpass
The crystal and the silver, pure
  As clearest polish'd glass.

Bedeckèd is the sapphire arch
  With streaks of scarlet hue ;
And preciously from end to end
  Damaskèd white and blue.

Calm is the deep and purple sea,
  Yea, smoother than the sand ;
The waves, that weltering wont to be,
  Are stable like the land.

The ships becalmed upon the seas,
  Hang up their sails to dry ;
The herds, beneath their leafy trees,
  Amidst the flowers they lie.

The little busy humming bees,
  That never think to drone,
On flowers and flourishes of trees
  Collect their liquor brown.

The dove with whistling wings so blue,
  The winds can fast collect,
Her purple pens turn many a hue
  Against the sun direct.

Great is the calm, for everywhere
  The wind is setting down,
The smoke goes upright in the air,
  From every tower and town.

What pleasure then to walk, and see,
　Along a river clear,
The perfect form of every tree
　Within the deep appear.

The bells and circles on the waves,
　From leaping of the trout,
The salmon from their holes and caves
　Come gliding in and out.

O sure it were a seemly thing,
　While all is still, and calm,
The praise of God to pray, and sing,
　With trumpet, and with shawm.

All labourers draw home at even,
　And can to other say,
" Thanks to the gracious God of Heaven,
　Who sent this summer's day."

A. Hume

[A Scotch poet of the middle of the sixteenth century.]

CCXVI
THE TURF SHALL BE MY FRAGRANT SHRINE

The turf shall be my fragrant shrine ;
My temple, Lord, that arch of Thine ;
My censer's breath the mountain airs,
And silent thoughts my only prayers.

My choir shall be the moonlit waves,
When murm'ring homeward to their caves,
Or when the stillness of the sea,
Ev'n more than music, breathes of Thee.

I'll seek by day some glade unknown,
All light and silence, like Thy throne!
And the pale stars shall be, at night,
The only eyes that watch my rite.

Thy Heaven, on which 'tis bliss to look,
Shall be my pure and shining book,
Where I shall read, in words of flame,
The glories of Thy wondrous name.

I'll read Thy anger in the rack
That clouds awhile the day-beam's track;
Thy mercy in the azure hue
Of sunny brightness breaking through!

There's nothing bright, above, below,
From flowers that bloom to stars that glow,
But in its light my soul can see
Some feature of Thy Deity!

There's nothing dark, below, above,
But in its gloom I trace Thy love,
And meekly wait that moment when
Thy touch shall turn all bright again!
T. Moore

CCXVII

HARVEST HOME

Come, ye thankful people, come,
Raise a song of harvest home!
All is safely gather'd in,
Ere the winter snows begin;

God, our Maker, doth provide
For our wants to be supplied;
Come to God's own temple, come,
Raise a song of harvest home!

We ourselves are God's own field,
Fruit unto His praise to yield;
Wheat and tares together sown,
Unto joy or sorrow grown;
First the blade, and then the ear,
Then the full corn shall appear;
Grant, O Harvest-Lord, that we
Wholesome grain and pure may be.

For the Lord our God shall come
And shall take His harvest home!
From His field shall purge away
All that doth offend that day;
Give His angels charge at last
In the fire the tares to cast,
But the fruitful ears to store
In His garner evermore.

Then thou Church triumphant, come,
Raise the song of harvest-home!
All are safely gather'd in,
Free from sorrow, free from sin;
There for ever purified,
In God's garner to abide.
Come, ten thousand angels, come,
Raise a glorious harvest home!

H. Alford

CCXVIII
JOY TAUGHT BY NATURE

The child leans on its parent's breast,
Leaves there its cares, and is at rest;
The bird sits singing by his nest,
        And tells aloud
His trust in God, and so is blest
        'Neath every cloud.

He has no store, he sows no seed;
Yet sings aloud, and doth not heed;
By flowing stream or grassy mead
        He sings to shame
Men who forget, in fear of need,
        A Father's name.

The heart that trusts for ever sings,
And feels as light as it had wings;
A well of peace within it springs,
        Come good or ill:
Whate'er to-day, to-morrow, brings,
        It is His will!
                 I. Williams

CCXIX
WAVES AND LEAVES

    Waves, waves, waves!
Graceful arches lit with night's pale gold,
Boom like thunder through the mountains roll'd,
Hiss and make their music manifold,
    Sing and work for God along the strand.

Leaves, leaves, leaves !
Beautified by Autumn's scorching breath,
Ivory skeletons carven fair by death,
   Float and drift at a sublime command.

Thoughts, thoughts, thoughts !
Rolling wave-like on the mind's strange shore,
Rustling leaf-like through it evermore,
   O that they might follow God's good Hand !
William Alexander

CCXX

THE RAINBOW

Triumphal arch, that fill'st the sky
   When storms prepare to part,
I ask not proud philosophy
   To teach me what thou art.

Still seem as to my childhood's sight,
   A midway station given,
For happy spirits to alight
   Betwixt the earth and heaven.

Can all that optics teach, unfold
   Thy form to please me so
As when I dreamt of gems and gold
   Hid in thy radiant bow ?

When Science from Creation's face
   Enchantment's veil withdraws,
What lovely visions yield their place
   To cold material laws !

And yet, fair bow, no fabling dreams,
   But words of the Most High,
Have told why first thy robe of beams
   Was woven in the sky.

When o'er the green undelug'd earth
   Heaven's covenant thou didst shine,
How came the world's grey fathers forth
   To watch thy sacred sign!

And when its yellow lustre smil'd
   On mountains yet untrod,
Each mother held aloft her child,
   To bless the bow of God.

Methinks thy jubilee to keep
   The first-made anthem rang
On earth deliver'd from the deep,
   And the first poet sang.

Nor ever shall the Muse's eye
   Unraptur'd greet thy beam;
Theme of primeval prophecy,
   Be still the poet's theme.

The earth to thee its incense yields,
   The lark thy welcome sings,
When glittering in the freshen'd fields
   The snowy mushroom springs.

How glorious is thy girdle cast
   O'er mountain, tower, and town,
Or mirror'd in the ocean vast,
   A thousand fathom down.

As fresh in yon horizon dark,
  As young thy beauties seem,
As when the eagle from the ark
  First sported in thy beam.

For faithful to its sacred page,
  Heaven still rebuilds thy span,
Nor lets the type grow pale with age,
  That first spoke peace to man.

T. Campbell

CCXXI

THE WILD FOWL'S VOICE

It chanced upon the merry merry Christmas eve,
I went sighing past the church across the moorland
    dreary—
  O! never sin and want and woe this earth will
      leave,
And the bells but mock the wailing sound, they sing
    so cheery.

  How long, O Lord! how long, before Thou come
      again?
Still in cellar, and in garret, and on mountain
    dreary,
  The orphans moan, and widows weep, and poor
      men toil in vain,
Till earth is sick of hope deferr'd, though Christmas
    bells be cheery.

Then arose a joyous clamour, from the wild fowl
    on the mere,
Beneath the stars, across the snow, like clear bells
    ringing,
And a voice within cried—" Listen !—Christmas
    carols even here
Though thou be dumb, yet o'er their work, the stars
    and snows are singing.

Blind !—I live, I love, I reign ; and all the nations
    through,
With the thunder of My judgments even now are
    ringing ;
Do thou fulfil thy work, but as yon wild fowl do,
Thou wilt heed no less the wailing, yet hear through
    it angels singing."

C Kingsley

CCXXII

ROBIN REDBREAST

Sweet Robin, I have heard them say,
That thou wert there upon the day,
That Christ was crown'd in cruel scorn :
And bore away one bleeding thorn,
That so, the blush upon thy breast,
In shameful sorrow was imprest :
And thence thy genial sympathy,
With our redeemed humanity.

Sweet Robin, would that I might be
Bath'd in my Saviour's blood, like thee ;
Bear in my breast, whate'er the loss,
The bleeding blazon of the cross ;

Live ever, with thy loving mind,
In fellowship with human kind;
And take my pattern still from thee,
In gentleness and constancy.

Bishop Doane

CCXXIII
THE SEA-BIRD.

Sea-bird! haunter of the wave,
   Delighting o'er its crest to hover;
Half engulphed where yawns the cave
   The billow forms in rolling over;
Sea-bird! seeker of the storm!
   In its shriek thou dost rejoice;
Sending from thy bosom warm
   Answer shriller than its voice.

Bird of nervous wingèd flight,
   Flashing silvery to the sun,
Sporting with the sea-foam white,
   When will thy wild course be done?
Whither tends it? Has the shore
   No alluring haunt for thee?
Nook with tangled vines grown o'er,
   Scented shrub, or leafy tree?

Is the purple sea-weed rarer
   Than the violet of the spring?
Is the snowy foam wreath fairer
   Than the apple's blossoming?

Shady grove and sunny slope—
  Seek but these, and thou shalt meet
Birds not born with storm to cope,
  Hermits of retirement sweet.

Where no winds too rudely swell,
  But in whispers, as they pass,
Of the fragrant flow'ret tell,
  Hidden in the tender grass.
There the mock-bird sings of love;
  There the robin builds his nest;
There the gentle-hearted dove,
  Brooding, takes her blissful rest.

Sea-bird, stay thy rapid flight:
  Gone! where dark waves foam and dash,
Like a lone star on the night—
  Far I see his white wing flash.
He obeyeth God's behest,
  All their destiny fulfil:
Tempests some are born to breast—
  Some to worship, and be still.

If I struggle with the storm
  On life's ever-changing sea,
Where cold mists enwrap the form,
  My harsh destiny must be.
Sea-bird! thus may I abide
  Cheerful the allotment given,
And, rising o'er the ruffled tide,
  Escape, at last, like thee, to heaven?

A. M. Wells

CCXXIV

THE LEGEND OF THE CROSSBILL

From the German

On the cross the dying Saviour
   Heavenward lifts his eyelids calm,
Feels, but scarcely feels, a trembling
   In His pierced and bleeding palm.

And by all the world forsaken,
   Sees He how with zealous care,
At the ruthless nail of iron,
   A little bird is striving there.

Stain'd with blood, and never tiring,
   With its beak it doth not cease;
From the Cross 'twould free the Saviour,—
   Its Creator's Son release.

And the Saviour speaks in mildness:
   " Blest be thou of all the good!
Bear as tokens of this moment
   Marks of blood and holy rood!"

And that bird is call'd the crossbill,
   Cover'd all with blood so clear,
In the groves of pine it singeth
   Songs, like legends, strange to hear.

H. W. Longfellow

CCXXV

MY DOVES

My little doves have left a nest
   Upon an Indian tree,
Whose leaves fantastic take their rest
   Or motion from the sea:
For ever there the sea-winds go
With sunlit paces, to and fro.

The tropic flowers look'd up to it,
   The tropic stars look'd down:
And there my little doves did sit
   With feathers softly brown,
And glittering eyes that show'd their right
To general Nature's deep delight.

And God them taught at every close
   Of water far, and wind
And lifted leaf, to interpose
   Their chanting voices kind;
Interpreting that love must be
The meaning of the earth and sea.

My little doves were borne away
   From that glad nest of theirs;
Across an ocean foaming aye,
   And tempest-clouded airs.
My little doves! who lately knew
The sky and wave by warmth and blue!

And now within the city prison,
   In mist and chillness pent,
With sudden upward look they listen
   For sounds of past content—
For lapse of water, swell of breeze,
Or nut-fruit falling from the trees.

The stir, without the glow of passion,
   The triumph of the mart—
The gold and silver's dreary clashing
   With man's metallic heart—
The wheelèd pomp, the pauper tread,
These only sounds are heard instead.

Yet still, as on my human hand
   Their fearless heads they lean,
And almost seem to understand
   What human musings mean,—
With such a plaintive gaze, their eyne
Are fasten'd upwardly to mine.

Their chant is soft as on the nest
   Beneath the sunny sky,
For love that stirred it in their breast
   Remains undyingly,
And 'neath the city's shade can keep
The well of music clear and deep.

And love, that keeps the music, fills
   With pastoral memories;
All echoings from out the hills,
   All droppings from the skies,
All flowings from the wave, and wind,
Remember'd in their chant I find.

So teach ye me the wisest part,
   My little doves ! to move
Along the city ways with heart
   Assured by holy love,
And vocal with such songs as own
A fountain to the world unknown.

'Twas hard to sing by Babel's stream,
   More hard in Babel's street !
But, if the soulless creatures deem
   Their music not unmeet,
For sunless walls,—let us begin,
Who wear immortal wings within !

To me fair memories belong
   Of scenes that erst did bless ;
For no regret—but present song—
   And lasting thankfulness—
And very soon to break away
Like types, in purer things than they !

I will have hopes that cannot fade,
   For flowers the valley yields ;
I will have humble thoughts instead
   Of silent dewy fields !
My spirit and my God shall be
My sea-ward hill, my boundless sea.

                      E. B. Browning

CCXXVI
TO A SKYLARK

Ethereal minstrel, pilgrim of the sky,
  Dost thou despise the earth where cares abound?
Or, while thy wings aspire, are heart and eye
  Both with thy nest upon the dewy ground?
Thy nest which thou canst drop into at will,
Those quivering wings composed, that music still.

Leave to the nightingale her shady wood;
  A privacy of glorious light is thine;
Whence thou dost pour upon the world a flood
  Of harmony, with instinct more divine;
Type of the wise, who soar, but never roam;
True to the kindred points of Heaven and Home.
William Wordsworth

CCXXVII
TO THE FIRST SWALLOW

'Tis not one blossom makes a spring,
  Nor yet one swallow makes a summer;
But a sweet promise both may bring,
  And thine is sweet, thou glad new comer!

Thy twittering voice, thy pinions light,
  That glance, and glide with fleetest motion,
Unwearied, though but yesternight
  They buoy'd thee o'er the wide-spread ocean,—

A welcome promise bring once more
  Of sparkling waters, waving meadows,
And countless things that fleet before
  My spirit's eye in glimmering shadows;—

Till gazing on thee wheeling near,
  And hailing thee with joyful bosom,
I know not whether is more dear,
  The summer bird, or vernal blossom.

The blossom brought a promise sweet,
  Sweet too is thine, thou glad new-comer!
And I will joy, though pinions fleet
  Too aptly tell of joys in summer!

Too aptly?—Nay that word recall:
  Deem rather it were cause for weeping,
If pleasant summer days were all,
  And never came a day of reaping.

Or mark the swift-wing'd foreigner
  Again ; and check each thought of sadness :
All here may fade : it grieves not her :
  She knows another land of gladness.
                              T. Davis

CCXXVIII

THE LOSS OF THE FAVOURITE

The skylark has perceiv'd his prison door
  Unclosed ; for liberty the captive tries:
Puss eagerly hath watch'd him from the floor,
  And in her grasp he flutters, pants, and dies.

Lucy's own puss, and Lucy's own dear bird,
  Her foster'd favourites both for many a day,
That which the tender-hearted girl preferr'd,
  She, in her fondness, knew not sooth to say.

For if the skylark's pipe were shrill, and strong,
    And its rich tones the thrilling ear might please,
Yet pussy well could breathe a fireside song
    As winning, when she lay on Lucy's knees.

Both knew her voice, and each alike would seek
    Her eye, her smile, her fondling touch to gain;
How faintly then may words her sorrow speak,
    When by the one she sees the other slain.

Come, Lucy, let me dry those tearful eyes;
    Take thou, dear child, a lesson not unholy,
From one whom nature taught to moralize
    Both in his mirth, and in his melancholy.

I will not warn thee not to set thine heart
    Too fondly upon perishable things;
In vain the earnest preacher spends his art
    Upon that theme: in vain the poet sings.

It is our nature's strong necessity,
    And this the soul's unerring instincts tell:
Therefore I say, let us love worthily,
    Dear child, and then we cannot love too well.

Better it is all losses to deplore
    Which dutiful affection can sustain,
Than that the heart should, in its inmost core,
    Harden without it, and have lived in vain.

This love which thou hast lavish'd, and the woe
    Which makes thy lip now quiver with distress,
Are but a vent, an innocent o'erflow,
    From the deep springs of female tenderness.

And something I would teach thee from the grief
  That thus has fill'd those gentle eyes with tears,
The which may be thy sober, sure relief,
  When sorrow visits thee in after years.

I ask not whither is the spirit flown
  That lit the eye which there in death is seal'd;
Our Father hath not made that mystery known;
  Needless the knowledge, therefore not reveal'd.

But didst thou know in sure and sacred truth,
  It had a place assign'd in yonder skies,
There, through an endless life of joyous youth,
  To warble in the bowers of Paradise;

Lucy, if then the power to thee were given
  In that cold form its life to re-engage,
Wouldst thou call back the warbler from its Heaven,
  To be again the tenant of a cage?

Only that thou might'st cherish it again,
  Wouldst thou the object of thy love recall
To mortal life, and chance, and change, and pain.
  And death; which must be suffer'd once by all?

O, no, thou say'st: O, surely not, not so,
  I read the answer which those looks express:
For pure and and true affection, well I know,
  Leaves in the heart no room for selfishness.

Such love of all our virtues is the gem;
  We bring with us th' immortal seed at birth:
Of Heaven it is, and heavenly; woe to them
  Who make it wholly earthly, and of earth!

What we love perfectly, for its own sake
   We love and not our own, being ready thus
Whate'er self-sacrifice is ask'd, to make ;
   That which is best for it, is best for us.
O Lucy, treasure up that pious thought !
   It hath a balm for sorrow's deadliest darts ;
And with true comfort thou wilt find it fraught,
   If grief should reach thee in thy heart of hearts.
                                              R. Southey

CCXXIX

LESSON FROM NATURE

When my breast labours with oppressive care,
And o'er my cheek descends the falling tear,
While all my warring passions are at strife,
O ! let me listen to the words of life.
Raptures deep felt His doctrine did impart,
And thus He raised from earth the drooping heart.
Think not when all your scanty stores afford
Is spread at once upon the sparing board ;
Think not, when worn the homely robe appears,
While on the roof the howling tempest bears,
What farther shall this feeble life sustain,
And what shall clothe these shivering limbs again ?
Say, does not life its nourishment exceed ?
And the fair body its investing weed ?

   Behold ! and look away your low despair—
See the light tenants of the barren air ;
To them nor stores, nor granaries belong,
Nought but the woodland, and the pleasing song ;
Yet your kind Heavenly Father bends His eye
On the least wing that flits along the sky.

To Him they sing, when Spring renews the plain,
To Him they cry in Winter's pinching reign,
Nor is their music nor their plaint in vain :
He hears the gay, and the distressful call,
And with unsparing bounty fills them all.

Observe the rising lily's snowy grace,
Observe the various vegetable race ;
They neither toil, nor spin, but careless grow,
Yet see how warm they blush ! how bright they glow !
What regal vestments can with them compare !
What king so shining ! or what queen so fair !
If, ceaseless, thus the fowls of heaven he feeds,
If o'er the fields such lurid robes He spreads,
Will He not care for you, ye faithless ! say,
Is He unwise ? or are ye less than they ?

J. Thomson

CCXXX

THE CHILD TAUGHT FROM NATURE

O rich the tint of earthly gold,
   And keen the diamond's spark,
But the young lamb of Jesu's fold
   Should other splendours mark.

To soothe him in th' unquiet night,
   I ask no taper's gleam,
But bring him where th' aerial light
   Falls from the moon's soft beam.

His heart at early morn to store
   With fancies fresh and rare,
Count not thy jewels o'er and o'er,
   Show him no mirror's glare.

But lift him where the eastern heaven
    Glows with the sun unseen,
Where the strong wings to morning given
    Brood o'er a world serene.

Yet, might I choose a time, me seems
    That earliest wistful gaze
Were best to meet the softening beams
    Of sunset's glowing maze.

Wide be the western casement thrown
    At sultry evening's fall,
The gorgeous lines be duly shown
    That weave Heaven's wondrous pall.

Calm be his sleep, whose eyelids close
    Upon so fair a sight:
Not gentler mother's music flows
    Her sweetest, best good night.

                      J. Keble

CCXXXI

GOD'S PRESENCE IN NATURE

Almighty Father! . . .
                The rolling year
Is full of Thee. Forth in the pleasing Spring
Thy beauty walks, Thy tenderness, and love.
Wide flush the fields; the softening air is balm;
Echo the mountains round; the forest smiles;
And every sense, and every heart is joy.
Then comes thy glory in the summer months,
With light and heat refulgent: Then Thy sun

Shoots full perfection through the swelling year ;
And oft Thy voice in dreadful thunder speaks,
And oft at dawn, deep noon, or falling eve,
By brooks, and groves, in hollow whispering gales ;
Thy bounty shines in autumn unconfin'd,
And spreads a common feast for all that lives.
In winter, awful Thou ! with clouds and storms
Around Thee thrown ! tempest o'er tempest roll'd
Majestic darkness ! on the whirlwind's wing
Riding sublime, Thou bidst the world adore,
And tremblest Nature with Thy northern blast.

Should fate command me to the furthest verge
Of the green earth, to distant barbarous climes,
Rivers unknown to song, where first the sun
Gilds Indian mountains, or his setting beam
Flames on th' Atlantic isles, 'tis nought to me ;
Since God is ever present, ever felt,
In the void waste, as in the city full !
And where He vital breathes there must be joy.
When e'en, at last, the solemn hour shall come,
And wing my mystic flight to future worlds,
I cheerful will obey ; there with new powers,
With rising wonders, sing. I cannot go
Where universal love not shines around,
Sustaining all yon orbs, and all their suns,
From seeming evil still educing good,
And better theme again, and better still,
In infinite progression. But I lose
Myself in Him, in Light ineffable !
Come, then, expressive silence ! muse His praise.
J. Thomson

CCXXXII

VAGUE HOPES OF NATURE

Hope springs eternal in the human breast:
Man never is, but always to be blest.
The soul, uneasy, and confined from home,
Rests and expatiates in a world to come.
Lo, the poor Indian! whose untutor'd mind
Sees God in clouds, or hears Him in the wind;
His soul proud Science never taught to stray
Far as the solar walk, or milky way;
Yet simple nature to his hope has given,
Behind the cloud-topp'd hill, an humbler heaven;
Some safer world in depth of woods embrac'd,
Some happier island in the watery waste,
Where slaves once more their native land behold,
No fiends torment, no Christians thirst for gold.
To *be*, contents his natural desire,—
He asks no angel's wing, no seraph's fire;
But thinks, admitted to that equal sky,
His faithful dog shall bear him company.
A. Pope

CCXXXIII

FLOWERS

Sweet nurslings of the vernal skies,
  Bath'd in soft airs, and fed with dew,
What more than magic in you lies
  To fill the heart's fond view?

In childhood's sports companions gay;
In sorrow, on life's downward way,
How soothing! in our last decay,
  Memorials prompt and true.
Relics ye are of Eden's bowers,
  As pure, as fragrant, and as fair,
As when ye crown'd the sunshine hours
  Of happy wanderers there.
Fall'n all beside—the world of life,
How is it stain'd with fear and strife!
In reason's world what storms are rife,
  What passions rage and glare!
But cheerful, and unchanged the while,
  Your first and perfect form ye show,
The same that won Eve's matron smile
  In the world's opening glow.
The stars of Heaven a course are taught,
Too high above our human thought;—
Ye may be found, if ye are sought,
  And as we gaze, we know.
Ye dwell beside our paths, and homes,
  Our paths of sin, our homes of sorrow
And guilty man, where'er he roams,
  Your innocent mirth may borrow.
The birds of air before us fleet,
They cannot brook our shame to meet—
But we may taste your solace sweet,
  And come again to-morrow.
Ye fearless in your nests abide;
  Nor may we scorn, too proudly wise,
Your silent lessons, undescried
  By all but lowly eyes;

For ye could draw th' admiring gaze
Of Him who worlds and hearts surveys;
Your order wild, your fragrant maze,
  He taught us how to prize.

Ye felt your Maker's smile that hour,
  As when He paused, and own'd you good,
His blessing on earth's primal bower,
  Ye felt it all renew'd.
What care ye now, if winter's storm
Sweep restless o'er each silken form?
Christ's blessing at your heart is warm,
  Ye fear no vexing mood.

Alas! of thousand bosoms kind,
  That daily court you, and caress,
How few the happy secret find
  Of your calm loveliness!
"Live for to-day!" to-morrow's light
To-morrow's cares shall bring to sight.
Go, sleep like closing flowers at night,
  And Heaven thy morn will bless.

J. Keble

CCXXXIV

THE BEACON

The scene was more beautiful far to my eye,
  Than if day in its pride had array'd it,
The land breeze blew mild, and the azure arch'd sky
  Look'd pure as the Spirit that made it.

The murmur rose soft as I silently gaz'd
On the shadowy waves' playful motion,
From the dim distant isle till the beacon-fire blaz'd
Like a star in the midst of the ocean.

No longer the joy of the sailor-boy's breast
Was heard in his wildly-breath'd numbers ;
The sea-bird had flown to her wave-girdled nest,
The fisherman sunk to his slumbers.

I sigh'd as I look'd from the hill's gentle slope ;
All hush'd was the billow's commotion ;
And I thought that the beacon look'd lovely as Hope,
That star of life's tremulous ocean.

The time is long past, and the scene is afar,
Yet, when my head rests on its pillow,
Will memory sometimes rekindle the star,
That blaz'd on the breast of the billow.

In life's closing hour, when the trembling soul flies,
And death stills the heart's last emotion,
O then may the seraph of mercy arise
Like a star on eternity's ocean.
T. Moore

CCXXXV

STAFFA

Merrily, merrily, goes the bark,
On a breeze from the northward free,
So shoots through the morning sky the lark,
Or the swan through the summer sea.

The shores of Mull on the eastward lay,
And Ulva dark, and Colonsay,
And all the group of islets gay
   That guard famed Staffa round.
Then all unknown its columns rose,
Where dark and undisturb'd repose
   The cormorant had found ;
And the shy seal had quiet home,
And welter'd in that wondrous dome,
Where, as to shame the temples deck'd
By skill of earthly architect,
Nature herself, it seem'd, would raise
A minster to her Maker's praise !
Not for a meaner use ascend
Her columns, or her arches bend ;
Nor of a theme less solemn tells
That mighty surge that ebbs and swells,
And still, between each awful pause,
From the high vault an answer draws,
In varied tone prolong'd and high,
That mocks the organ's melody.
Nor doth its entrance front in vain
To old Iona's holy fane,
That Nature's voice might seem to say,
" Well hast thou done, frail child of clay !
Thy humble powers that stately shrine
Task'd high, and hard—but witness mine."
Sir Walter Scott

CCXXXVI
THE STORM

The tempest rages wild, and high
The waves lift up their voice, and cry
Fierce answers to the angry sky,—
   Miserere Domine.
Through the black night, and driving rain,
A ship is struggling, all in vain,
To live upon the stormy main ;—
   Miserere Domine.
The thunders roar, the lightnings glare,
Vain is it now to strive or dare ;
A cry goes up of great despair,—
   Miserere Domine.
The stormy voices of the main,
The moaning wind, and melting rain
Beat on the nursery window pane :—
   Miserere Domine.
Warm curtain'd was the little bed,
Soft pillow'd was the little head,
"The storm will wake the child," they said :—
   Miserere Domine.
Cowering among his pillows white,
He prays, his blue eyes dim with fright,
"Father, save those at sea to-night!"
   Miserere Domine.
The morning shone, all clear and gay,
On a ship at anchor in the bay,
And on a little child at play.—
   Gloria tibi Domine!
    A. A. Proctor

CCXXXVII

SAND OF THE DESERT IN AN HOUR GLASS

A handful of red sand, from the hot clime
   Of Arab deserts brought,
Within this glass becomes the spy of Time,
   The minister of thought.

How many weary centuries has it been
   About those deserts blown !
How many strange vicissitudes has seen,
   How many histories known !

Perhaps the camels of the Ishmaelite
   Trampled, and pass'd it o'er
When into Egypt, from the patriarch's sight,
   His favourite son they bore.

Perhaps the feet of Moses, burnt and bare,
   Crush'd it beneath their tread ;
Or Pharaoh's flashing wheels into the air
   Scatter'd it as they sped ;

Or Mary, with the Christ of Nazareth
   Held close in her caress,
Whose pilgrimage of hope, and love, and faith,
   Illumed the wilderness ;

Or anchorites beneath Engeddi's palms,
   Pacing the Dead Sea beach,
And singing slow their old Armenian psalms
   In half articulate speech ;

Or caravans that from Bassora's gate
  With westward steps depart ;
Or Mecca's pilgrims, confident of fate,
  And resolute of heart.

These have pass'd over it, or may have pass'd !
  Now in this crystal tower
Imprison'd by some curious hand at last,
  It counts the passing hour.

And, as I gaze, these narrow walls expand ;—
  Before my dreamy eye
Stretches the desert with its shifting sand,
  Its unimpeded sky.

And borne aloft by the sustaining blast,
  This little golden thread
Dilates into a column, high and vast,
  A form of fear and dread.

And onward, and across the setting sun,
  Across the burning plain
The column and its broader shadow run
  Till thought pursues in vain.

The vision vanishes ! these walls again
  Shut out the lurid sun,
Shut out the hot immeasurable plain ;
  The half-hour's sand is run !

H. W. Longfellow

CCXXXVIII
A SUNDAY SCENE

A chapel, like a wild bird's nest,
Closely embower'd and trimly drest;
And thither young and old repair,
This sabbath-day, for praise and prayer.
Fast the churchyard fills;—anon
Look again, and they all are gone;
And scarcely have they disappear'd
Ere the prelusive hymn is heard:—
With one consent the people rejoice,
Filling the church with a lofty voice!
They sing a service which they feel:
For 'tis the sunrise now of zeal;
Of a pure faith, the vernal prime—
In great Eliza's golden time.
A moment ends the fervent din,
And all is hush'd, without and within;
For, though the priest, more tranquilly,
Recites the holy liturgy,
The only voice which you can hear
Is the river murmuring near.
When—soft!—the dusky trees between,
And down the path through the open green,
Where is no living thing to be seen;
And through yon gateway, where is found
Beneath the arch with ivy bound,
Free entrance to the church-yard ground—
Comes gliding in with lovely gleam,
Comes gliding in, serene and slow,
Soft and silent as a dream,
   A solitary doe!

White she is, as lily of June,
And beauteous as the silver moon
When out of sight the clouds are driven,
And she is left alone in Heaven ;
Or like a ship some gentle day,
In sunshine sailing far away,
A glittering ship, that hath the plain
Of ocean for her own domain.

Beside the ridge of a grassy grave
In quietness she lays her down ;
Gentle as a weary wave
Sinks, when the summer breeze has died,
Against an anchor'd vessel's side ;
Even so, without distress, doth she
Lie down in peace, and lovingly.

The day is placid in its going,
To a lingering motion bound,
Like the crystal stream now flowing
With its softest summer sound :
So the balmy minutes pass,
While this radiant creature lies
Couched upon the dewy grass,
Pensively with downcast eyes.
— But now again the people raise,
With awful cheer a voice of praise ;
It is the last, the parting song ;
And from the temple forth they throng,
And quickly spread themselves abroad,
While each pursues his several road.
But some—a variegated band
Of middle aged, and old, and young,

And little children by the hand
Upon their leading mothers hung,—
With mute obeisance gladly paid,
Turn toward the spot, where, full in view,
The white doe, to her service true,
   Her sabbath couch hath made.
" Look, there she is, my child ! draw near;
She fears not, wherefore should we fear?
She means no harm ;" but still the boy,
To whom the words were softly said,
Hung back, and smiled, and blush'd for joy.
A shamfaced blush of glowing red !
Again the mother whisper'd low,
" Now, you have seen the famous doe ;
From Rylstone she hath found her way
Over the hills this sabbath day ;
Her work, whate'er it be, is done,
And she will depart when we are gone ;
Thus doth she keep, from year to year,
Her sabbath morning, foul or fair."
W. Wordsworth

CCXXXIX

BROUGH BELLS

One day to Helbeck I had stroll'd
   Among the Crossfell hills,
And resting in its rocky grove,
   Sat listening to the rills ;
The while, to their sweet undersong,
   The birds sang blithe around,
And the soft west wind awoke the wood
   To an intermitting sound.

Louder or fainter, as it rose
    Or died away, was borne
The harmony of merry bells
    From Brough that pleasant morn.

" Why are the merry bells of Brough,
    My friend, so few ? " said I,
" They disappoint th' expectant ear
    Which they should gratify.

" One, two, three, four ; one, two, three, four ;
    'Tis still one, two, three, four ;
Mellow and silvery are the tones,
    But I wish the bells were more ! "

" What, art thou critical ? " quoth he ;
    " Eschew that heart's disease
That seeketh for displeasure
    Where the intent hath been to please.

" By those four bells there hangs a tale,
    Which, being told, I guess,
Will make thee hear their scanty peal
    With proper thankfulness.

" Not by the Cliffords were they given,
    Nor by the Tufton's line ;
Thou hearest in that peal the crune
    Of old John Brunskill's kine.

" On Stanemore's side, one summer eve,
    John Brunskill sate to see,
His herds in yonder Borrodaile
    Come winding up the lea.

"Behind them, on the lowland's verge,
    In the evening light serene;
Brough's silent tower, then newly built
    By Blenkinsop, was seen.

"Slowly they came in long array,
    With loitering pace at will:
At times a low from them was heard,
    Far off, for all was still.

"The hills returned that lonely sound
    Upon the tranquil air;
The only sound it was, which then
    Awoke the echoes there.

"'Thou hear'st that lordly bull of mine,
    Neighbour,' quoth Brunskill then;
'How loudly to the hills he crunes,
    That crune to him again?

"'Think'st thou, if yon whole herd at once
    Their voices should combine,
Were they at Brough, that we might not
Hear plainly from this upland spot
    That cruning of the kine?'

"'That were a crune, indeed,' replied
    His comrade, 'which, I ween,
Might at the Spital well be heard,
    And in all dales between.

"'Up Mallerstang to Eden's springs
The eastern wind upon its wings
    The mighty voice could bear;
And Appleby would hear the sound,
    Methinks, when skies are fair.

"'Then shall the herd,' John Brunskill cried,
  'From yon dumb steeple crune,
And thou, and I, on this hill side
  Will listen to their tune.'

"So, while the merry bells of Brough
  For many an age ring on,
John Brunskill will remember'd be,
  When he is dead and gone;

"As one who in his later years,
  Contented with enough,
Gave freely what he well could spare
  To buy the bells of Brough.

"Thus it hath proved: three hundred years
  Since these have passed away,
And Brunskill's is a living name
  Remember'd to this day."

"More pleasure," I returned, "shall I
  From this time forth partake,
When I remember Helbeck woods,
  For old John Brunskill's sake.

"He knew how wholesome it would be
  Among these wild wide fells,
And upland vales, to catch at time
  The sound of Christian bells;

"What feelings, and what impulses
  That cadence might convey
To herdsman, or to shepherd boy,
Whiling in indolent employ
  The solitary day;

" That when his brethren were convened
   To meet for social prayer,
He too, admonish'd by the call,
   In spirit might be there.

" Or when a glad thanksgiving sound,
   Upon the winds of heaven,
Was sent to speak a nation's joy,
   For some great blessing given—

" For victory by sea or land,
   And happy peace at length;
Peace by his country's valour won,
   And 'stablish'd by her strength.

" When such exultant peals were borne
   Upon the mountain air,
The sound should stir his blood, and give
   An English impulse there."

Such thoughts were in the old man's mind,
   When he that eve look'd down
From Stanemore's side, on Borrodaile,
   And on the distant town.

And had I store of wealth, methinks,
   Another herd of kine,
John Brunskill, I would freely give,
   That they may crune with thine.

R. Southey

CCXL

TO THE WIND IN AN EOLIAN HARP

Ethereal race, inhabitants of air,
Who hymn your God amid the secret grove,
Ye unseen beings, to my harp repair,
And raise majestic strains, or melt in love.

Those tender notes, how kindly they upbraid!
With what soft woe they thrill the listener's heart!
Sure from the hand of some unhappy maid,
Who died in youth, these sweet complainings part.

But hark! that strain was of a graver tone,
On the deep strings his hand some hermit throws;
Or he the sacred Bard who sat alone
In the drear waste, and wept his peoples' woes.

Such was the song which Zion's children sung,
When by Euphrates' stream they made their plaint;
And to such sadly solemn tones are strung
Angelic harps, to soothe a dying saint.

Methinks I hear the full celestial choir
Thro' heaven's high dome their awful anthem raise;
Now chanting clear, and now they all conspire
To swell the lofty hymn from praise to praise.

Let me, ye wand'ring spirits of the wind,
Who, as wild fancy prompts you, touch the string,
Smit with your theme, be in your chorus join'd,
For till you cease my muse forgets to sing.

J. Thomson

CCXLI

GOD IN NATURE AND GRACE

God is love; the heavens tell it
  Through their glorious orbs of light,
In that glad and golden language
  Speaking to us day and night,
    Their great story,
  God is love, and God is light.

And the teeming earth rejoices
  In that message from above,
With ten thousand thousand voices
  Telling back, from hill and grove,
    Her glad story,
  God is might, and God is love.

Through these anthems of creation,
  Struggling up with gentle strife,
Christian songs of Christ's salvation
  To the world, with blessings rife,
    Tell their story,
  God is love, and God is life.

Up to Him let each affection
  Duly rise, and round Him move;
Our whole lives one resurrection
  To the life of life above;
    Our glad story,
  God is life, and God is love.

Anon.

CCXLII

THE CREATION

All things bright and beautiful,
    All creatures, great and small,
All things wise and wonderful,
    The Lord God made them all.

Each little flower that opens,
    Each little bird that sings,
He made their glowing colours,
    He made their tiny wings;

The rich man in his castle,
    The poor man at his gate,
God made them, high or lowly,
    And order'd their estate.

The purple-headed mountain,
    The river running by,
The sunset, and the morning
    That brightens up the sky;

The cold wind in the winter,
    The pleasant summer sun,
The ripe fruits in the garden,—
    He made them every one.

The tall trees in the greenwood,
    The meadows where we play,
The rushes by the water
    We gather every day;—

He gave us eyes to see them,
And lips that we might tell
How great is God Almighty
Who has made all things well!

C. F. Alexander

LIST OF AUTHORS

ADAMS, Sarah F. XIX
ADDISON, Joseph, V, CCI
ALEXANDER, Cecil F. XXVIII, LXI, CCXLII
ALEXANDER, William, LXIX, CCXIX
ALFORD, Henry, CXV, CXLIX, CCXVII
ARNOLD, Mathew, CLIX, CLXXIII
AUSTIN, John, IX

BONAR, Horatio, CLXIX, CLXXVII
BROOME, William, LXVII
BROWNING, Elizabeth B. CLXXXIX, CCXXV
BURNS, Robert, CXXIV
BURRIDGE, Thomas, XXII
BYROM, John, CLXXXI
BYRON, Lord, LXV

CAMPBELL, Thomas, CCXX
CAREY, Phœbe, CXXXV
CASWALL, Edward, XV
COWLEY, Abraham, LIX, LXIII, CXLV
COWPER, William, VII, XXI, LXXXIII, C, CLII, CLXVI, CLXXVIII
COXE, Arthur Cleveland, CLXXIX
CRABBE, George, CX
CRASHAW, Richard, XXXIV, CXLVI
CROSSMAN, Samuel, CXXXII

DAVIS, Thomas, XCVII, XCVIII, CCXXVII
DAVISON, John, CXLIV
DE VERE, Aubrey, CLXX, CXCVII, CCXIII, CCXIV
DOANE, Bishop, CCXXII
DRYDEN, John, LIII, LXXXIX, CXXX

EDMESTON, James, CXXXIV
ELLIOTT, Charlotte, CLXXXII, CLXXXVII, CXCII

FABER, Frederic W. XLI, CXLIII, CLXXI, CLXXII

GOLDSMITH, Oliver, CXXV
GRANT, Sir Robert, XLIII
GRIGG, Joseph, CLXVIII
GURNEY, John Hampden, IV

HASTINGS, Thomas, CLXXXVI, CXCVI
HEBER, Bishop Reginald, XXV, XXXVI, CXXXIX, CCIV, CCVII
HEMANS, Felicia, CXIII, CLVIII, CCV
HERBERT, George, XLVIII, LXXXI, XCV, XCVI, CXII
HERRICK, Robert, XXIII, CXXIX
HOWE, William Walsham, XXXIX
HOWITT, Mary, CXI
HUME, Alexander, CCXV

INGELOW, Jean, CLX, CLXI

JONSON, Ben, VI, XXXII, XCIV
JUDSON, Emily, CXX

KEBLE, John, XVII, LVIII, LX, LXIV, LXXIII, LXXXIV, CVI, CVII, CIX,
  CLIV, CLXXIV, CLXXV, CCXXX, CXXXIII
KELLY, Thomas, CXXXII
KEN, Bishop Thomas, XXIX
KINGSLEY, Charles, CIII, CCXXI

LITTLEWOOD, William E. LXXVI, LXXVII, LXXVIII, LXXX, CCII
LOGAN, John, LII, LXVI
LONGFELLOW, Henry Wadsworth, LXXXVII, CXXXVII, CXLVIII, CLV,
  CLVI, CCXXIV, CXXXVII
LOWELL, James R. CXCIX
LYNCH, Anne C. XXXVIII
LYTE, Henry F. CLXXXVIII

MACARTHY, Dennis F. CCXI, CCXII
MACLEOD, Norman, CXXVII
MARVEL, Andrew, VIII
MASSEY, Gerald, CLXV
McCHEYNE, Robert M. LXXII
MILMAN, Henry Hart, XXX, XL, XLII, CXL
MILNES, R. M. CV, CLXIII
MILTON, John, XXVI, XXVII, CXXXVIII
MONSELL, John S. CXC
MONTGOMERY, James, I, III
MOORE, Henry, XXXI, L
MOORE, Thomas, X, CXXI, CCIII, CCXVI, CCXXXIV
MOULTRIE, John, XLVII, CL

NEWMAN, John Henry, LXII
NEWTON, John, LI

OSGOOD, Frances S. CVIII

PALGRAVE, Francis T. XLIV
POPE, Alexander, XXXVII, CXXXVI, CXCV, CXCVIII, CCXXXII
PRIOR, Matthew, LXXXVIII
PROCTER, Adelaide Anne, XX, CCXXXVI

RALEIGH, Sir Walter, XCII
READ, Thomas B. CCX

SCOTT, Sir Walter, CCXXXV
SEARS, Edmund H. LXX
SHAKSPEARE, William, XC
SIGOURNEY, Louisa H. XCIX
SMITH, Alexander, CLXII, CXCIV
SOUTHEY, Caroline, CXVII
SOUTHEY, Robert, XI, CXLII, CLXXVI, CCXXVIII, CCXXXIX
SOUTHWELL, Robert, CI, CLXXXV
SPENSER, Edmund, LXXXV
STANLEY, Arthur Penrhyn, XLIX

TENNYSON, Alfred, XXXIII, LIV, LXXIV, LXXV, LXXIX, CLIII, CLXIV, CC
THOMSON, James, CCXXIX, CCXXXI, CCXL
TICKELL, Thomas, CXLVII
TOPLADY, Augustus M. XLVI
TRENCH, Archbishop, XXXV, CXXII, CXXIII, CLI, CLVII

VAUGHAN, Henry, CII, CXCI

WATTS, Isaac, XLV, CLXXXIII
WALLER, Edmund, CXIX
WARING, Anna Lætitia, XII
WASTELL, Samuel, CXXVIII
WELLS, Anna M. CCXXIII
WESLEY, Charles, XIV, CXXXIII
WHITE, Henry Kirke, LXXI, CIV
WHITTIER, John G. CXVIII
WHYTEHEAD, Thomas, LV, LVI, LVII
WILBERFORCE, Bishop, CLXX
WILLIAMS, Isaac, CXLI, CCXVIII
WILLIS, Nathaniel P. CCVI
WILSON, Professor, CXXXI
WITHER, George, II, CXIV
WORDSWORTH, William, XIII, XVI, CCVIII, CCIX, CCXXVI, CCXXXVIII
WOTTON, Sir Henry, XCIII

YOUNG, Edward, LXVIII, CLXXXIV

ANONYMOUS, XVIII, LXXXVII, CXVI, CXCIII, CCXLI
DITTO, Child's Christian Year, CLXVII
DITTO, Old Hymn, XCI
DITTO, from Ordination Service, XXIV

INDEX TO FIRST LINES

	Page
Abide with me! fast falls the even-tide	238
A chapel, like a wild bird's nest	298
A handful of red sand, from the hot clime	296
Alas! what secret tears are shed	129
All is o'er;—the pain—the sorrow	52
All things bright and beautiful	307
Almighty Father!	288
An ardent spirit dwells with Christian love	128
And is there care in Heaven, and is there love	98
And so the Word had breath, and wrought	62
As precious gums are not for lasting fire	156
As the hardy oat is growing	264
As grew the power of sacred lays	110
A song of a boat	199
Beautiful are the heralds	253
Behold! a stranger's at the door!	218
Behold the sun, that seem'd but now	132
Behold yon wretch, by impious passion driven	249
Beneath the chancel's hallow'd stone	173
Blest be Thy love, dear Lord	10
Bound upon th' accursèd tree	45
Brother, thou art gone before us	168
But let my due feet never fail	30
But on before me swept the moonlit stream	82
By cool Siloam's shady rill	40
By Nebo's lonely mountain	73
Calm me, my God, and keep me calm	257
Calm on the bosom of thy God	197
Child, amidst the flowers at play	131
Child of sin and sorrow	247
Christ before thy door is waiting	126
Come, Holy Ghost, our souls inspire	27
Come, my way, my truth, my life	95
Come, O! come, with sacred lays	2
Come, ye thankful people, come	269
Courage, brother, do not stumble	153
Courage, O faithful heart	90
Deep on the convent-roof the snows	250
Dim—as the borrow'd beams of moon and stars	62
Dying, still slowly dying	163

	Page
Eighteen hundred years agone	42
Ere last year's moon had left the sky	139
Ethereal race, inhabitants of air	305
Ethereal minstrel, pilgrim of the sky	282
Far away where the tempests play	93
Far from the world, O Lord, I flee	228
Father, I know that all my life	12
For Thou wert born of woman! Thou didst come	33
Gently speak and lightly tread	195
Give me a tender spotless child	124
Give me my scallop shell of quiet	112
Gloomy night embraced the place	36
Glory to Thee, my God, this night	31
God is love; the heavens tell it	306
God is ascended up on high	58
God moves in a mysterious way	8
God scatters love on every side	249
Going home from the House of God	99
Happy soul! thy days are ended	161
Hark! hark! my soul! angelic songs are swelling	221
Hark, my soul! it is the Lord	216
Hast thou seen with flash incessant	260
Hear me, O God	7
He is gone beyond—the skies	57
Her eyes are homes of silent prayer	89
He stopp'd at last	71
He, Who on earth as man was known	59
Holy, holy, holy, Lord	4
Holy! holy! holy! Lord God Almighty	28
Hope springs eternal in the human breast	290
How blest Thy creature is, O God	24
How happy is he born and taught	112
How pleasant to me thy deep blue wave	85
If Heavenly flowers might bloom unharm'd on earth	173
If you're waking, call me early, call me early, mother dear	207
I got me flowers to strew Thy way	56
I heard the voice of Jesus say	219
I hear thee speak of the better land	256
I look'd with pride on what I'd done	246
I mourn no more my vanish'd years	136
In pride, in reasoning pride our error lies	246
In the hour of my distress	26
In the hour of trial	21
In the silent midnight watches	229
In the days of our forefathers, the gallant days of old	146
Into a desolate land	92
In token that thou shalt not fear	133
I praised the earth, in beauty seen	255

Index

	Page
I say to thee—Do thou repeat	141
Is Resignation's lesson hard?	233
I sing the birth was born to-night	35
It came upon the midnight clear	83
It chanced upon the merry merry Christmas eve	274
It is not growing like a tree	113
Jesu! bless our slender boat	19
Jesus, my strength, my hope	16
Jesu, the very thought of Thee	18
Just as I am, without one plea	237
Late, late, so late! and dark the night, and chill	93
Latest born of Jesse's race	76
Launch thy bark, mariner! Christian, Heaven speed thee	135
Let me be with Thee where Thou art	231
Let other thoughts, where'er I roam	205
Let us quit the leafy arbour	259
Little pomp or earthly state	37
Like as the damask rose you see	155
Look westward, pensive little one	226
Lord Jesu, when we stand afar	44
Lord, with what care hast thou begirt us round	114
Lord! who art merciful as well as just	12
Lost! lost! lost!	117
Love thy God, and love Him only	230
Merrily, merrily, goes the bark	293
Methought I heard a sound, methought it came	203
My conscience is my crown	235
My fairest child, I have no song to give you	120
My God, my Father, while I stray	243
My life's a shade, my days	159
My little doves have left a nest	279
My soul, there is a country	243
My spirit longs for Thee	231
Nearer, my God, to Thee	22
Near yonder copse, where once the garden smiled	144
O come and mourn with me awhile	46
O day most calm, most bright!	130
O, fairest flower! no sooner blown but blasted	166
Of all the thoughts of God that are	239
O, happy is the man who hears	80
O happy soul, that lives on high	232
O Lord! how happy should we be	217
O miserable man	171
Once more, through God's high will and grace	265
One day to Helbeck I had stroll'd	300
On the cross the dying Saviour	278
O Paradise! O Paradise!	222

316   Index

	Page
O rich the tint of earthly gold	287
O, shame upon thee, listless heart	225
Oh that those lips had language! Life has pass'd	184
O Thou that driest the mourner's tear	11
Pause not to dream of the future before us	125
Poor little Willie	214
Praise be Thine, most Holy Spirit	25
Prayer is the soul's sincere desire	1
Receive him, earth, unto thine harbouring shrine	170
Religion does not censure or exclude	118
Return, O wanderer, to thy home	236
Rise, crown'd with light, imperial Salem rise	41
Robert of Sicily, brother of Pope Urbane	103
Rock of Ages, cleft for me	51
Sabbath of the saints of old	66
Saviour, when in dust to Thee	48
Say, watchman, what of the night?	134
Sea-bird! haunter of the wave	276
She had been told that God made all the stars	257
Slowly fashioned, link by link	115
Some murmur when their sky is clear	140
Soon and for ever	241
So rest, for ever rest, O Princely Pair!	197
Star of morn and even	50
Summer is a glorious season	262
Sun of my soul, Thou Saviour dear	20
Sweet day, so calm, so cool, so bright	114
Sweet maiden, for so calm a life	190
Sweet nurslings of the vernal skies	290
Sweet Robin, I have heard them say	275
Take them, O Death! and bear away	176
The air of death breathes through our souls	157
The Assyrian came down like the wolf on the fold	79
The child leans on its parent's breast	271
The cloud-capp'd towers, the gorgeous palaces	110
The day is cloudy; it should be so	171
The flower is small that decks the field	116
The Holy Son of God most high	34
The lights o'er yonder snowy range	264
The Lord my pasture shall prepare	6
The roseate hues of early dawn	80
The sea of Fortune doth not even flow	119
The seas are quiet when the winds are o'er	138
The scene was more beautiful far to my eye	292
The skylark has perceiv'd his prison door	282
The spacious firmament on high	252
The stars shine bright while earth is dark	247
The time draws near the birth of Christ	86

	Page
The time so tranquil is, and clear	266
The turf shall be my fragrant shrine	268
The tempest rages wild, and high	295
The way is long and dreary	23
The yellow poplar leaves came down	201
Then constant faith, and holy hope shall die	109
There is a fountain fill'd with blood	96
There is a Reaper, whose name is Death	165
There is a thought so purely blest	122
There is no flock, however watch'd and tended	193
There is no love like the love of Jesus	94
They sin who tell us love can die	226
This world I deem	63
This world is all a fleeting show	140
Thou art gone to the grave! but we will not deplore thee	167
Thou art, O God! the life and light	254
Thou canst accomplish all things, Lord of might	82
Thou spakest and the waters roll'd	65
Thou wert fair, Lady Mary	177
Thou, who dost dwell alone	223
Thou whom chance may hither lead	142
Through sorrow's path, and danger's road	121
Through the love of God, our Saviour	245
'Tis folly all that can be said	174
'Tis not one blossom makes a spring	282
—To our high-raised phantasy present	29
To these, whom death again did wed	174
Triumphal arch, that fill'st the sky	272
Vital spark of heavenly flame	164
Waves, waves, waves!	271
We beside the wondrous river	72
We have lost him; he is gone!	188
We've no abiding city here	95
We walk'd within the churchyard bounds	182
What is good for a bootless bene?	14
What is the Church, and what am I?	123
What mourner ever felt poetic fire?	175
What though my harp and viol be	156
When brothers part for manhood's race	87
When first thine eyes unveil, give thy soul leave	120
When I survey the wondrous cross	51
When Lazarus left his charnel-cave	89
When marshall'd on the nightly plain	84
When my breast labours with oppressive care	286
When our heads are bow'd in woe	47
When Spring unlocks the flowers to paint the laughing soil	258
When the great Hebrew king did almost strain	77
When the hours of Day are number'd	192
Where high the heavenly temple stands	61

	Page
Where the remote Bermudas ride	9
Which is the happiest death to die	161
While snows even from the mild south-west	68
Who for the like of me will care?	78
Who has this Book and reads it not	111
Within this leaf to every eye	220
Yes, God is good: in earth and sky	5
Yes, so it was ere Jesus came	98
Yes, surely there's a love abroad	261
Yet though the fig-tree should no burden bear	81

RICHARD CLAY AND SONS, LONDON AND BUNGAY.